KETO SNACKS

SWEET AND DELICIOUS KETOGENIC & LOW-CARB DIET - A SIMPLE KETO DIET COOKBOOK FOR BEGINNERS

By Anthony Taylor & Jenny Taylor

© **Copyright 2019 - All rights reserved.**

The content contained within this book may not be reproduced, duplicated or transmitted without direct written permission from the author or the publisher.

Under no circumstances will any blame or legal responsibility be held against the publisher, or author, for any damages, reparation, or monetary loss due to the information contained within this book. Either directly or indirectly.

Legal Notice:

This book is copyright protected. This book is only for personal use. You cannot amend, distribute, sell, use, quote or paraphrase any part, or the content within this book, without the consent of the author or publisher.

Disclaimer Notice:

Please note the information contained within this document is for educational and entertainment purposes only. All effort has been executed to present accurate, up to date, and reliable, complete information. No warranties of any kind are declared or implied. Readers acknowledge that the author is not engaging in the rendering of legal, financial, medical or professional advice. The content within this book has been derived from various sources. Please consult a licensed professional before attempting any techniques outlined in this book.

By reading this document, the reader agrees that under no circumstances is the author responsible for any losses, direct or indirect, which are incurred as a result of the use of information contained within this document, including, but not limited to, — errors, omissions, or inaccuracies.

Table of Contents

INTRODUCTION VIII

CHAPTER 1 BASIC ELEMENTS OF THE KETO DIET 1
   BULLETPROOF COFFEE 10

CHAPTER 2 DELICIOUS KETO SALTY & SPICY SNACKS 11
   CRUNCHY SNACKS 11
      Air Fried - Bacon-Wrapped Chicken 11
      Avocado Tuna Melt Bites 13
      Bacon Cheddar Cheese Crisps 14
      Bacon Cucumber Bites 15
      Bacon Pickle Fries 17
      Bacon-Wrapped Mushrooms 18
      Broiled Bacon Wraps with Dates 19
      Cheese Chips 20
      Chicken on A Skewer 21
      Chocolate Dipped Candied Bacon 23
      Fried Queso Fresco 24
      Garlic Bread 25
      Garlic Parmesan Fried Eggplant 27
      Grain-Free Philly Cheesesteak Stuffed Peppers 28
      Olive Cheese Balls 30
      Parmesan Chips 32
      Peanut Butter Power Granola 33
      Roasted Pumpkin Seeds 34
      Tomato Chips 36
      Tortilla Chips 37

   TASTY DIPS & SAUCES FOR SNACK TIME 38
      Avocado Ranch Dip 38
      Blue Cheese Dip/Dressing 40
      Chili Dip 41
      Creamy Avocado Cilantro Lime Dressing 42
      Eggplant Dip 43
      5-Layer Mexican Dip Bowls You Can Eat with A Fork 45
      Guacamole 46
      Keto-Friendly Mayonnaise 47
      Olive Spread with Pecans 48
      Ranch Dip 49
      Ranch Seasoning 50
      Spicy Keto Pimento Cheese 51

   PIZZA & QUICHE TIME 52

- Bell Pepper Pizza ... 52
- Cheese & Almond Pizza ... 54
- Mini Crustless Quiche ... 55
- Pita Pizza ... 56
- Pizza Bites ... 57
- Sausage & Salsa Quiche ... 59
- Smoked Sausage & Swiss Cheese Quiche ... 60
- Zucchini Pizza Bites ... 61
- Tacos & Wraps for Fun ... 62
- Avocado & Salmon Omelet Wrap ... 63
- BLT Wrap ... 64
- Chipotle Fish Tacos ... 65
- Coleslaw Stuffed Wraps ... 67

DELICIOUS APPETIZERS ... 68
- Caprese Snacks ... 68
- Salmon & Cream Cheese Bites ... 69

CHAPTER 3 FAT BOMB FAVORITES ... 70
- Cheesy Bacon Bombs ... 70
- Pizza Fat Bombs ... 72
- Stuffed Pecan Fat Bombs ... 73

KETO SWEET BOMBS ... 74
- Almond & Allspice Fat Bombs ... 74
- Almond Butter Fat Bombs ... 75
- Blackberry Coconut Fat Bombs ... 76
- Blueberry Frozen Fat Bombs ... 77
- Chocolate Fat Bombs ... 78
- Chocolate & PB Avocado Pudding Bomb ... 79
- Chocolate & Peppermint Bombs ... 80
- Cinnamon & Cardamom Fat Bombs ... 81
- Coconut & Cinnamon Bombs ... 82
- Coconut Orange Creamsicle Fat Bombs ... 83
- Coffee Fat Bombs ... 86
- Dark Chocolate Fat Bombs ... 87
- Neapolitan Fat Bombs ... 88
- No-Bake Lemon Cheesecake Fat Bombs ... 89
- Pistachio & Almond Fat Bombs ... 90

CHAPTER 4 HIGH-FAT KETO SNACKS FOR VEGETARIANS ... 92

VEGETARIAN-FRIENDLY KETOGENIC BEVERAGES ... 94
- Coffee & Cream ... 94
- Hot Chocolate ... 95
- Pumpkin Spice Latte ... 96
- Vanilla Coffee & Whipped Cream ... 98

KETO SNACKS

DELICIOUS VEGETARIAN SNACKS **99**
    Cheese Puffs *99*
    Cheese Roll-Ups *100*
    Keto Bread Twists *101*
    Keto Spicy Roasted Nuts *103*
    Roasted Almonds *104*
    Slow-Roasted Cashews *105*
    Sun-Dried Tomato Pesto Mug Cake *106*

SWEET VEGETARIAN SNACKS **107**
    Chia Raspberry Pudding *107*
    Choco Mug Brownie *109*
    Chocolate & Hazelnut Spread *110*
    Cinnamon Coconut Chips *111*
    Coffee Cake *112*
    Crunchy Berry Mousse *114*
    Keto Brunch Brownies *115*
    Peanut Butter Fudge *116*
    Pistachio Ice Cream *118*
    White Chocolate Fat Bomb - Vegetarian *119*

CHAPTER 5 DELICIOUS SMOOTHIES & FROZEN TREATS FOR SNACKS **120**
    Almond & Blueberry Smoothie *120*
    Almond Strawberry Smoothie *122*
    Avocado Mint Green Smoothie *123*
    Avocado Raspberry Smoothie *124*
    Blackberry Cheesecake Smoothie *125*
    Blackcurrant Smoothie *126*
    Blueberry Smoothie *127*
    Blueberry - Banana Bread Smoothie *129*
    Blueberry - Chia & Coconut Smoothie *130*
    Blueberry Yogurt Smoothie *131*
    Chocolate Smoothie *132*
    Chocolate Mint Smoothie *133*
    Chocolate & Raspberry Cheesecake Smoothie *134*
    Cinnamon Smoothie *135*
    Cinnamon Chocolate Smoothie *136*
    Cucumber & Spinach Smoothie *137*
    Easter Smoothie *139*
    Mexican Chocolate Smoothie *140*
    St. Patrick's Day Smoothie *141*
    Strawberry Smoothie *142*
    Strawberry & Rhubarb Pie Smoothie *144*
    Tropical Smoothie *145*

FROZEN TREATS **146**
    Cheesecake Popsicles *146*

KETO SNACKS

- Chocolate Bon-bons ... 147

CHAPTER 6 SWEET & TASTY KETO RECIPES FOR DESERTS ... 148

PUDDING & MOUSSE OPTIONS ... 148
- Almond Pumpkin Pudding ... 148
- Cheesecake Pudding ... 150
- Chia Pudding ... 151
- Lemon Custard ... 152

COOKIES ... 153
- Almond Nut Butter Cookies ... 153
- Amaretti Cookies ... 154
- Chocolate Chip Cookies ... 155
- Chocolate Coconut Cookies ... 157
- Cinnamon Cookies ... 158
- Delicious Homemade Graham Crackers ... 159
- Ginger Snap Cookies ... 161
- Macaroons ... 162
- Orange Walnut Cookies ... 163
- P B & J Cookies ... 164
- Pistachio Cookies ... 165
- Walnut Cookies ... 166

MUFFINS ... 167
- Apple Cinnamon Muffins ... 167
- Brownie Muffins ... 168
- One-Minute Muffin ... 169
- Pumpkin Maple Flaxseed Muffins ... 170

PIES ... 172
- Blueberry Cream Pie ... 172
- Creamy Lime Pie ... 174
- Mini Coconut Pies ... 176
- Pumpkin Cheesecake Pie ... 178

OTHER DELICIOUS SWEET TREATS ... 180
- Almond Chia Bars ... 180
- Apple Cider Donut Bites ... 182
- Baked Apples ... 184
- Baked Brie & Almonds ... 185
- Blueberry Tart ... 186
- Cheesecake Cupcakes ... 187
- Cheesecake Mocha Bars ... 188
- Coconut Bars ... 190
- Coconut & Chocolate Bites ... 191
- Coconut Cream Brownies ... 192
- Cream Cheese Truffles ... 194

KETO SNACKS

Peanut Butter & Coconut Balls *195*
Pumpkin Bars with Cream Cheese Frosting *196*
Pumpkin Blondies *198*
Strawberry & Cream Cakes *199*
Strawberry Gummies *201*
Strawberry Rhubarb Crumble *202*
White Chocolate Bark *205*

CHAPTER 7 TIPS TO REMAIN IN KETOSIS **207**

CONCLUSION **212**

INTRODUCTION

Congratulations on purchasing your personal copy of the *Keto Snacks: Sweet and Delicious Ketogenic & Low-Carb Diet – A Simple Keto Diet Cookbook For Beginners*. Thank you for doing so.

A ketogenic diet will help you reduce your calorie intake to below the volume of calories your body can consume each day. It's essential to summon the energy stockpiled in the fat cells to deliver fuel or power to your muscles. This is accomplished through the dieting technique used by the keto diet which will limit the volume of carbs you consume.

A substantial percentage of your fuel for the day will come from fat transformed to ketones. Once you have the protein, carbohydrates, and fat ratio monitored by the diet plan; you are well on the way to a successful diet strategy. You won't be over-eating with large portions of protein. You also won't eliminate fat or carbs which make it a safe diet plan for fat loss.

If you take the approach of eating less, without considering your diet—you'll be losing essential minerals and vitamins you need daily—which can result in muscle spasms, fatigue, mental fogginess, hunger, headaches, irritability, insomnia, and emotional depression. You can also lose valuable muscle mass; not just the pounds you intended to drop.

By using the low-carb keto plan, you can reduce your carbohydrates, calorie counts, and nurture your body with the suitable amount of water, meat, eggs, fish, veggies, nuts, as well as high-quality oils which create fat loss minus the unpleasant side effects.

Not only will you lose weight, but you will also lower your triglycerides, blood pressure, and blood sugar. There's no set rule for carb intake. These are the basic guidelines to consider as you blaze the path on the ketogenic diet plan:

- *20-50 Grams Each Day:* If you have diabetes, are obese, or metabolically deranged, this is the plan for you. Your body will achieve a ketosis state which supplies the ketone bodies.

- *100-150 Grams Each Day:* Stay within these limits if you are active and lean trying to maintain weight.

As you now see, it is important to experiment and categorize where you fall on the scales before you make any changes. As with any new diet changes, you should seek your doctor's advice.

KETO SNACKS

CHAPTER 1

BASIC ELEMENTS OF THE KETO DIET

You will soon realize the keto diet is flexible - yet strict. Each individual will lose weight differently, and other people may not have the same goals as you. For now, as a beginner, you will be using the first method. These are four unique plans, so you better understand the different levels:

Ketogenic Technique # 1: The standard ketogenic diet (SKD) consists of moderate protein, high-fat, and is low in carbs.

Ketogenic Technique # 2: Workout times will call for the targeted keto diet, which is also called TKD. The process consists of adding additional carbohydrates to the diet plan during the times when you are more active.

Ketogenic Technique # 3: The cyclical ketogenic diet (CKD) entails a restricted five-day keto diet plan followed by two high-carbohydrate days.

Ketogenic Technique # 4: The high-protein keto diet is comparable to the standard keto plan (SKD) in all aspects, except you will consume more protein.

Vital Roles Played By Protein & Carbs

Each of the nutrients plays an essential role in your health.

Importance of Protein

If you're looking for an effective keto plan, protein is a must for your diet, including saving your calories, as a fat burner, and to help repair your muscles. In particular:

Repair in muscle and growth: Taking protein on days you're more active is more effective. Understanding the balance of fats, proteins and carbs is very vital. Balancing these will help you in your keto diet.

Protein Help Burn Calories: Consuming protein help slow down the digestion process and make you feel more satisfied. At the beginning, it's important to feel full so you won't cheat with your selections.

Protein Burns Fat: With the help of carbs or protein, it's easier to burn fat quicker. Balancing protein is essential to preserve your lean muscles.

Carbohydrates

Carbs are exchanged into glucose giving us an energy boost. Roughly half of our calorie's intake is produced by carbs which store as glycogen. When needed, it releases from the body.

Creating adenosine triphosphate (ATP) require glucose. Glucose help fuel the body and is important for daily maintenance. After liver reach its limit, carbs turn to fat.

The Difference between a Low-Carb & Ketogenic Diet Plan

There is a difference between a low-carb diet and the keto diet. Low carb diet will average roughly around 100 grams of carbs. The long-term of the diet may differ substantially depending on the number of fats and proteins that are consumed. Each of the recipes in this book is balanced by the ketogenic standards, so you can decide on your carb intake daily.

Good Fat vs. Bad Fat

The Good Fats:

Add Extra-Virgin Olive Oil (EVOO): Olive oil dates back for centuries to a time where oil was used for anointing kings and priests. It's a high-quality oil maintaining low-acidity which makes this oil have a smoke point as high as 410° Fahrenheit. That's higher than most cooking applications call for, making olive oil more heat-stable than many other cooking fats. It contains zero carbs for two teaspoons.

Monounsaturated fats, such as the ones in olive oil, are also linked with better blood sugar regulation, including lower fasting glucose, as well as reducing inflammation throughout the body. Olive oil also helps to prevent cardiovascular disease by protecting the integrity of your vascular system and lowering LDL which is also called your 'bad' cholesterol.

Add Macadamia Oil: One of the benefits of this oil is that it has a high smoke point of 390° Fahrenheit. It carries a mild flavor which is a super alternative for olive oil in mayonnaise.

Other Healthy Monounsaturated and Saturated Fats

Include these items (listed per net carbs and shown <u>in grams</u>):

- Olives – 3 jumbo - 5 large or 10 small (1)
- Avocado oil – 1 tbsp. (0)
- Sesame oil – 1 tbsp. (0)
- Chicken fat – 1 tbsp. (0)
- Duck Fat – 1 tbsp. (0)
- Beef Tallow – 1 tbsp. (0)
- Flaxseed oil – 1 tbsp.(0)
- Unsweetened flaked coconut – 3 tbsp. (2)
- Unsalted Butter – 1 tbsp. (0)
- Ghee - 1 tsp. (0)
- Egg yolks – 1 large (0.6)
- Organic red palm oil - 1 tbsp. (0)
- Keto-friendly mayonnaise

The Limited "Bad" Fats:

You need to be aware of unhealthy processed trans fats and polyunsaturated fats. These fats are acquired through processing and are found in foods including fast foods, crackers, margarine, and cookies. Avoid canola, soybean, safflower, and cottonseed vegetable oils. If it was processed in a factory and prepackaged; you need to be aware of its fat content.

Ingredient Essential for the Ketogenic Diet

Stock the Pantry

KETO SNACKS

You want your ingredients to be keto-friendly. Begin with these items:

- Coconut flour
- Quinoa
- Splenda & Stevia
- Sugar-free ketchup
- Sugar-free gelatin
- Unsweetened cocoa powder
- Yellow mustard
- Pickles (limit sweet or bread & butter)
- Natural nut butter – no sugar

Stock Up On Healthy Protein Products

The keto plan focuses on quality proteins, not carbohydrates. You will see many items listed as a starting point for your snacks:

- Tuna: Fresh & Canned
- Salmon: Fresh wild caught salmon – portioned in bags to freeze
- Eggs
- Shrimp
- Fresh nuts: Macadamia, sesame seeds, flax seeds, chia seeds, etc.
- Turkey: Breasts & ground turkey
- Pork Chops
- Chicken: Thighs, breasts, drumsticks, & ground chicken
- Beef: Flank steak, chuck roast, sirloin, lean ground beef
- Venison: This is an excellent choice since it is lean, as well as vegetarian-raised meat.

Stock Up On Healthy Fresh Fruits

Fruits are excellent snack foods. Each of the following is portioned for .5 cup servings or 100 grams:

- Apples – no skin - boiled – 13.6 total carbs

KETO SNACKS

- Apricots - 7.5 total carbs
- Bananas - 23.4 total carbs
- Fresh Blackberries - 5.4 net carbs
- Fresh Blueberries - 8.2 net carbs
- Fresh Strawberries - 3 net carbs
- Cantaloupe - 6 total carbs
- Raw Cranberries - 4 net carbs
- Gooseberries - 8.8 net carbs
- Kiwi – 14.2 total carbs
- Fresh Boysenberries - 8.8 net carbs
- Oranges – 11.7 total carbs
- Peaches - 11.6 total carbs
- Pears – 19.2 total carbs
- Pineapple - 11 total carbs
- Plums – 16.3 total carbs
- Watermelon- 7.1 total carbs

Consider These Spices:

Make Your Homemade Pumpkin Pie Spice:

Use this simple low-carb concoction, and you know it will be healthy.

Servings: 10.75 tsp.
Total Macros per 1 tsp. serving:
- .8 g Net Carbs
- .09 g Fat
- .12 g Protein
- 6.42 Calories

Ingredients:

- Ground cinnamon (2 tbsp.)
- Ground nutmeg (.5 tsp.)
- Ground ginger (1 tbsp.)
- Allspice (.5 tsp.)

- Cardamom (.25 tsp.)
- Ground cloves (.5 tsp. or .75 tsp. whole cloves)

Preparation Instructions:

1. Use a spice grinder to grind the cloves into powder.
2. Combine all of the components into a large mixing container until combined thoroughly.
3. Store in a spice container to use any time the need arises.

Cinnamon (6 grams per (1) tablespoon) Use cinnamon as part of your daily plan to improve your insulin receptor activity. Just add one-half of a teaspoon of cinnamon into a smoothie, shake, or any other keto dessert. As you will observe, many of the keto recipes contain the ingredient.

Consider these as well:

- *Thyme* (0.2 grams per tsp.)
- *Garlic Powder* (7 grams per 1 tbsp.)
- *Nutmeg* (3.5 grams per 1 tbsp.)
- *Paprika* (3.7 grams per 1 tbsp.)
- *Dill Seed* (3.6 grams per 1 tbsp.)

Wisely Choose Your Sweeteners

- Stevia Drops offer flavors including English toffee, hazelnut, vanilla, and chocolate. You can make sweetened coffee or drinks quickly. However, everyone is different, and some think the drops are bitter to taste. Therefore, only use three drops to equal one teaspoon of sugar.

- Xylitol has been added to the topside of the sugary list. It's excellent for sweetening your teriyaki or BBQ sauce, and it does taste like sugar! The natural-occurring sugar alcohol has the Glycemic index (GI) standing of 13. Some have reported a slightly minty aftertaste.

The xylitol is also known to keep your mouth bacteria in check and improving your dental health. It is commonly found in chewing gum. However, if used in large amounts, it can cause diarrhea.

- The best all-around sweetener is Pyure Organic All-Purpose Blend. There's no bitter aftertaste with this stevia-based product. The blend of stevia and erythritol is an excellent alternative to your sweetening, baking, and cooking needs. It is suggested that you substitute 1/3 teaspoon of Pyure for every one teaspoon of sugar. Adjust this to your taste, since you can always add a bit more.

    For powdered sugar, you can grind the sweetener in a NutriBullet or other blender until it's very dry.

- Swerve Granular Sweetener is also an excellent choice as a blend which is made from non-digestible carbs sourced from starchy root veggies and select fruits. It is an excellent choice for those who do not like the taste of stevia.

    Swerve is on the market as a one-to-one substitute. However, start with ¾ of a teaspoon for every one of sugar. Increase the portion as desired. Swerve also has its own confectioners/powdered sugar for your baking needs. On the downside, it is more expensive than other products such as the Pyure.

Tools Necessary

It is important to test your ketone levels to remain in ketosis. As the ketones are produced in the liver, the body is shifting its metabolism away from glucose and towards fat utilization. "Nutritional ketosis is defined by serum ketones ranging from 0.5 to 3.0 mm."

Use A Blood Ketone Meter: The ketone bodies beta-hydroxybutyrate or BHB is the most accurately measured using a blood ketone meter. The meter is pricey, but it's the most accurate tool.

Use Urine Ketone Strips: Uriscan and Ketostix are not as accurate as other methods. They can only measure acetoacetate levels. They are useful in the first phase of the diet when you are just seeking the carbohydrate levels to enter into ketosis. On the top side, they are simple to use and start at about $7 monthly for the strips.

Use the Ketonix Acetone Breathalyzer: Your acetone is tested using this cheaper alternative. However, breath ketones don't always correlate identically with blood ketones since they could be affected by alcohol consumption or the intake of water prior to testing times.

Are you a coffee lover? If you are, why not make a delicious cup of coffee before you begin?

Bulletproof Coffee

Servings: 1
Total Prep & Cook Time: 5 minutes
Total Macro Nutrients per Serving:
- -0- g Net Carbs
- 51 g Total Fats
- 1 g Total Protein
- 463 Calories

Fixings Needed:

- MCT oil powder (2 tbsp.)
- Ghee/butter (2 tbsp.)
- Hot coffee (1.5 cups)

Preparation Method:

1. Empty the hot coffee into your blender.
2. Pour in the powder and butter. Blend until frothy.
3. Enjoy in a large mug.

CHAPTER 2

DELICIOUS KETO SALTY & SPICY SNACKS

You will find many new snacks in this segment - from crackers to chicken - to take care of your cravings with simple recipes with each of the macros included.

Crunchy Snacks

Air Fried - Bacon-Wrapped Chicken

Servings: 3
Total Prep & Cook Time: 20 minutes
Total Macro Nutrients per Serving:
- .6 g Net Carbs
- 26.0 g Total Fats
- 31.0 g Total Protein
- 364 Calories

Fixings Needed:

- Breast of chicken (1)
- Unsmoked bacon (6 strips)
- Soft garlic cheese (1 tbsp.)

Preparation Method:

1. Slice the chicken into six pieces. Spread the garlic cheese over each bacon strip. Add a piece of chicken to each one.
2. Roll and secure with a toothpick.
3. Let the Air Fryer warm up for three to four minutes. Arrange the wraps in the hot fryer and cook 15 minutes for a quick snack any time.

Avocado Tuna Melt Bites

Servings: 12
Total Prep & Cook Time: 15 minutes
Total Macro Nutrients per Serving:

- 1.02 g Net Carbs
- 17.8 g Total Fats
- 5 g Total Protein
- 185 Calories

Fixings Needed:

- Mayonnaise (.25 cup)
- Parmesan cheese (.25 cup)
- Drained tuna (10 oz.)
- Almond flour (.33 cup)
- Onion powder (.25 tsp.)
- Garlic powder (.5 tsp.)
- Pepper and salt (to your liking)
- Cubed avocado (1 medium)
- Coconut oil for cooking (2 tbsp.)

Preparation Method:

1. Remove the pit from the avocado and cut into cubes.
2. Combine each of the fixings (omitting the oil and avocado).
3. Fold in the tuna with the avocado to form balls. Coat with the flour.
4. Warm up the oil using the medium temperature setting and fry until browned. Serve or store.

Bacon Cheddar Cheese Crisps

Servings: 3
Total Prep & Cook Time: 10 minutes
Total Macro Nutrients per Serving:
- 1.1 g Net Carbs
- 11.8 g Total Fats
- 0.7 g Total Protein
- 150 Calories

Fixings Needed:

- Cooked bacon (3 strips)
- Shredded cheddar cheese (1 cup)

Preparation Method:

1. Set the oven ahead of time to 350° Fahrenheit.
2. Prepare a baking tin with a sheet of parchment paper.
3. Pour about one tablespoon of the cheese onto the tray for each serving. Break the bacon to bits and add to the piles of cheese.
4. Bake for 5 to 8 minutes and let cool. Blot the grease away with a paper towel before serving.

Bacon Cucumber Bites

Servings: 4-6
Total Prep & Cook Time: 10 minutes
Total Macro Nutrients per Serving:
- 1.3 g Net Carbs
- 14 g Total Fats
- 0.9 g Total Protein
- 131 Calories

Fixings Needed:

- Cucumbers (2)
- Dill weed (1 tsp.)
- Chives (1 tbsp.)
- Onion (1 tbsp.)
- Bell pepper (1 tbsp.)
- Cream cheese (8 oz.)

Preparation Method:

1. Chop the onions, chives, and bell pepper. Take the cheese out of the fridge to soften. Cut the cucumbers into halves - lengthwise. Discard the seeds.
2. Combine the cream cheese with the dill weed, onions, peppers, and chives.
3. Fill each half with the cream cheese mixture.
4. Slice into 1-inch chunks for serving.

Bacon Knots

Servings: 4
Total Prep & Cook Time: 35 minutes
Total Macro Nutrients per Serving:
- 1.3 g Net Carbs
- 33 g Total Fats
- 30 g Total Protein
- 442 Calories

Fixings Needed:

- Raw bacon (16 slices)
- Shredded parmesan (.25 cup)
- Minced garlic (4 cloves)
- Minced parsley (1 tbsp.)
- Pepper & Salt (to taste)

Preparation Method:

1. Straighten one slice of bacon. Tie it into a knot.
2. Take another slice, and tie another knot around the first one. Continue until done.
3. Place the chain on a parchment-lined baking tin.
4. Warm up the oven to reach 400° Fahrenheit.
5. Sprinkle the bacon with the garlic and bake for 15 minutes.
6. When crispy, sprinkle with the parsley and cheese.
7. Bake for one more minute. Break apart and serve.

Bacon Pickle Fries

Servings: 12
Total Prep & Cook Time: 20 minutes
Total Macro Nutrients per Serving:
- 1.2 g Net Carbs
- 16 g Total Fats
- 2 g Total Protein
- 159 Calories

Fixings Needed:

- Bacon (12 slices)
- Pickle spears (12)
- Keto-friendly-Ranch dressing (.25 cup)

Preparation Method:

1. Warm up the oven to 425° Fahrenheit.
2. Prepare a baking tray with a layer of parchment paper.
3. Wrap each of the pickles with a piece of bacon and arrange on the baking sheet.
4. Bake until crispy or about 12 to 15 minutes. Turn after about 7 minutes.
5. Serve with your favorite ranch or other dressing.

Bacon-Wrapped Mushrooms

Servings: 12
Total Prep & Cook Time: 20 minutes
Total Macro Nutrients per Serving:
- 1.6 g Total Carbs
- 26.4 g Total Fats
- 8 g Total Protein
- 275 Calories

Fixings Needed:

- Strips of bacon (25)
- Portobello or white mushrooms (25)
- Black pepper & Salt (to your liking)
- Also Needed: Toothpicks

Preparation Method:

1. Warm up the oven to reach 400° Fahrenheit.
2. Remove the stems from the mushrooms and wrap each cap with a bacon strip. Securely close with the toothpick.
3. Arrange each of the prepared treats on the prepared pan.
4. Bake for 15 minutes. Place on paper towels to drain. Serve or store for later.

Broiled Bacon Wraps with Dates

Servings: 6
Total Prep & Cook Time: 55 minutes
Total Macro Nutrients per Serving:
- 5 g Total Carbs
- 10 g Total Fats
- 19 g Total Protein
- 203 Calories

Fixings Needed:

- Sliced bacon (1 lb.)
- Slit - pitted dates (8 oz.)

Preparation Method:

1. Warm up the oven to reach 425° Fahrenheit.
2. Use a ½ slice of the bacon and wrap each of the dates. Close with a toothpick.
3. Put the wraps on a baking tin. Bake for 15 to 20 minutes.
4. Serve.

Cheese Chips

Servings: 4
Total Prep & Cook Time: 10 minutes
Total Macro Nutrients per Serving:
- 0.1 g Net Carbs
- 16 g Total Fats
- 16 g Total Protein
- 191 Calories

Fixings Needed:

- Cheddar or Edam cheese slices (8 oz.)
- Hot paprika (.5 tsp.)

Preparation Method:

1. Set the oven temperature setting at 400° Fahrenheit.
2. Place the cheese slices on a parchment paper-lined baking tin.
3. Sprinkle with the paprika.
4. Bake for 8 to 10 minutes.

Chicken on A Skewer

Servings: 4
Total Prep & Cook Time: 30 minutes
Total Macro Nutrients per Serving:
- 4.5 g Net Carbs
- 12.3 g Total Fats
- 31.5 g Total Protein
- 259 Calories

Fixings Needed:

- White onion (1)
- Green pepper (1)
- Chicken fillet (15 oz. pkg.)
- Salt (1 tsp.)
- Stevia (1 tsp.)
- Paprika (1 tsp.)
- Coconut milk (1 tbsp.)
- Coconut oil (1 tbsp.)
- Apple cider vinegar (1 tbsp.)

Preparation Method:

1. Chop the chicken into bite-sized cubes and toss in with the salt, paprika, and vinegar. Let it absorb the spices for about 5 minutes.
2. Remove the seeds and roughly chop the green pepper. Pour in the olive oil.
3. Peel and roughly chop the onion. String the skewers with the meat, onions, and peppers.
4. Warm up the grill and cook the skewers for 15 minutes. Turn often and serve.

KETO SNACKS

Chocolate Dipped Candied Bacon

Servings: 16
Total Prep & Cook Time: 2 hours
Total Macro Nutrients per Serving:
- 1.1 g Net Carbs
- 4.1 g Total Fats
- 3 g Total Protein
- 54 Calories

Fixings Needed:

- Bacon (16 thin-cut slices)
- Brown sugar alternative – ex. Surkin Gold (2 tbsp.)
- Cinnamon (.5 tsp)
- Cacao butter (.5 oz.) or Coconut oil (1 tbsp.)
- 85% dark chocolate (3 oz.)
- Sugar-free maple extract (1 tsp.)

Preparation Method:

1. Mix the Surkin Gold with the cinnamon.
2. Lay the strips on a parchment paper-lined tray and sprinkle with about half of the mixture. Turn them over and do the other side with the rest of the mixture.
3. Heat up the oven until it reaches 275° Fahrenheit. Bake until caramelized and crispy (approximately 1 hour and 15 min.).
4. Warm up a pan to melt the cocoa butter and chocolate. Pour in the maple syrup and stir well. Set aside until it's room temperature.
5. Arrange the bacon on a platter to cool thoroughly before dipping into the chocolate.
6. Dip half of each strip of the bacon into the chocolate.
7. Arrange on a tray for the chocolate to solidify. You can place it in the refrigerator or just on the countertop.

Fried Queso Fresco

Servings: 5
Total Prep & Cook Time: 10-15 minutes
Total Macro Nutrients per Serving:
- 2.7 g Net Carbs
- 25.6 g Total Fats
- 16.4 g Total Protein
- 307 Calories

Fixings Needed

- Coconut oil (1 tbsp.)
- Queso fresco (1 lb.)
- Olive oil (.5 tbsp.)

Preparation Method:

1. Chop the cheese into cubes.
2. Heat both of the oils to the smoking point, and toss in the cheese.
3. Fry the cheese, flipping until well browned.
4. Remove and let the cheese rest to cool.
5. Drain on towels to remove the oil.

Garlic Bread

Servings: 20
Total Prep & Cook Time: 70 minutes
Total Macro Nutrients per Serving:
- 1 g Net Carbs
- 9 g Total Fats
- 2 g Total Protein
- 92 Calories

Fixings Needed:

- Almond flour (1.25 cups)
- Baking powder (2 tsp.)
- Ground psyllium husk powder (5 tbsp.)
- Sea salt (1 tsp.)
- White wine or cider vinegar (2 tsp.)
- Boiling water (1 cup)
- Egg whites (3)

Fixings Needed For The Garlic Butter:

- Butter - room temperature (4 oz.)
- Garlic clove (1 minced)
- Fresh parsley - finely chopped (2 tbsp.)
- Salt (.5 tsp.)

Preparation Method:

1. Warm up the oven to reach 350° Fahrenheit. Combine the dry fixings in a mixing container.
2. Start the pot of water. Once boiling, pour in the egg whites and vinegar. Whisk using a hand mixer for about 30 seconds.
3. Shape and roll into hot dog buns, leaving plenty of space to allow them to expand.
4. Bake using the lower rack for 40 to 50 minutes. When ready, remove to cool.
5. Prepare the garlic butter and chill.
6. Take the garlic butter out of the fridge. Slice the cooled buns using a serrated knife. Spread garlic butter on each half.
7. Reheat the oven to 425° Fahrenheit.
8. Bake until lightly browned (10 to 15 min.).

Garlic Parmesan Fried Eggplant

Servings: 6
Total Prep & Cook Time: 45-50 minutes
Total Macro Nutrients per Serving:
- 6 g Net Carbs
- 22 g Total Fats
- 12 g Total Protein
- 271 Calories

Fixings Needed:

- Large egg (1)
- Eggplant (1 medium)
- Garlic powder (2 tsp.)
- Salt divided (1 tsp.)
- Parmesan cheese (1 cup)
- Almond flour (1 cup)
- Coconut oil or butter (.5 cup)
- Pepper (.5 tsp.)

Preparation Method:

1. Slice the eggplant into 1/2-inch slices. Dust with .5 tsp. of the salt. Wait for about 30 minutes. Dab it dry using a paper towel and add to a baking sheet (single layered).
2. Whisk the egg in one bowl.
3. In another container, whisk the salt, pepper, garlic powder, parmesan, and almond flour.
4. Heat 1-2 tablespoons of butter/oil using the medium heat temperature setting.
5. Dip the slices of eggplant in the egg, shake off the excess, and dredge in the almond flour concoction. Shake off the excess.
6. Fry the prepared slices in a skillet, browning until each side is browned and crispy. Drain on towels before serving.

Grain-Free Philly Cheesesteak Stuffed Peppers

Servings: 4
Total Prep & Cook Time: 30 minutes
Total Macro Nutrients per Serving:
- 1 g Net Carbs
- 32 g Total Fats
- 20 g Total Protein
- 399 Calories

Fixings Needed:

- Green peppers (4)
- Butter (1 tbsp.)
- Chopped onions (.25 cup)
- Minced garlic (1 tsp.)
- Green peppers (.25 cup)
- Shaved beef steak (1 lb.)
- Salt & pepper (to taste) or Montreal steak seasoning
- Mayonnaise (2 tbsp.)
- Pepper jack cheese (7 slices)

Preparation Method:

1. Remove and chop the tops from the peppers and place into a 400° Fahrenheit oven.
2. Chop the onions and toss into a skillet with the butter, garlic, and (tops) chopped peppers. Sauté until softened.
3. Toss in the steak and seasonings of choice; chopping them apart as they cook. Add a slice of cheese and turn off the heat.
4. Transfer the peppers from the oven when softened just a little and stuff.
5. Add ½ of a slice of cheese to each of the pepper halves.
6. Add the mayonnaise to the steak and mix. Scoop into the pepper shells adding a piece of cheese to the top of all the stuffed peppers.
7. Broil until the cheese melts or about 5 minutes.

Olive Cheese Balls

Servings: 12
Total Prep & Cook Time: 20 minutes
Total Macro Nutrients per Serving:
- 5 g Total Carbs
- 8 g Total Fats
- 4 g Total Protein
- 110 Calories

Fixings Needed:

- Pimento stuffed olives (24)
- Shredded cheddar cheese (1 cup)
- Softened butter (2 tbsp.)
- Keto-friendly flour of choice - ex. coconut or almond (.5 cup)
- Cayenne pepper (as desired)

Preparation Method:

1. Warm up the oven to reach 400° Fahrenheit.
2. Combine the butter and cheese in a mixing container. Fold in the flour and mix combining with the pepper.
3. Wrap the mixture around each of the olives. Place on the cookie sheet.
4. Bake for about 15 minutes and serve or enjoy later.

KETO SNACKS

Parmesan Chips

Servings: 2
Total Prep & Cook Time: 15 minutes
Total Macro Nutrients per Serving:
- 3.7 g Net Carbs
- 18 g Total Fats
- 27.4 g Total Protein
- 277 Calories

Fixings Needed:

- Turmeric (.25 tsp.)
- Basil (.33 tsp.)
- Thyme (.5 tsp.)
- Paprika (.5 tsp.)
- Parmesan cheese (6 oz.)

Preparation Method:

1. Grate the cheese into a mixing container and sprinkle with the spices. Stir well.
2. Program the oven to 370° Fahrenheit. Cover a baking tray with parchment paper or foil.
3. Make the circles from the mixture and add to the prepared tray.
4. Bake for ten minutes and chill.
5. Serve hot or cold.

Peanut Butter Power Granola

Servings: 12
Total Prep & Cook Time: 40 minutes
Total Macro Nutrients per Serving:
- 4.75 g Net Carbs
- 30.1 g Total Fats
- 9.4 g Total Protein
- 338 Calories

Fixings Needed:

- Pecans (1.5 cups)
- Almonds (1.5 cups)
- Sunflower seeds (.25 cup)
- Almond flour or Shredded coconut (1 cup)
- Swerve sweetener (.33 cup)
- Vanilla whey protein powder (.33 cup)
- Butter (.25 cup)
- Peanut butter (.33 cup)
- Water (.25 cup)

Preparation Method:

1. Set the oven at 300° Fahrenheit.
2. Prepare a rimmed baking tin with a layer of parchment paper.
3. Process the almonds and pecans in a food processor and add to a large bowl.
4. Fold in the sunflower seeds, sweetener, shredded coconut, and protein powder.
5. Place the butter and peanut butter in the microwave to melt. Pour over the nut mixture. Toss lightly. Mix in the water.
6. Spread the mixture evenly onto the baking sheet.
7. Bake for 30 minutes. Stir about halfway through the cycle.
8. Cool before storing.

Roasted Pumpkin Seeds

Servings: 8
Total Prep & Cook Time: 70 minutes
Total Macro Nutrients per Serving - .25 cup serving:
- 6 g Net Carbs
- 25 g Total Fats
- 12 g Total Protein
- 305 Calories

Fixings Needed:

- Raw pumpkin seeds (2 cups)
- Garlic salt (1 tsp.)
- Ghee (1 tsp.)
- Coconut aminos (1 tsp.)
- Cumin (.25 tsp.)
- Paprika (.5 tsp.)

Preparation Method:

1. Warm up the oven to reach 300° Fahrenheit.
2. Combine the cumin, paprika, garlic salt, coconut aminos, and ghee, with the pumpkin seeds.
3. In a single layer, add the seeds and toss with the ghee/oil.
4. Bake until crispy or for about one hour.

Tomato Chips

Servings: 5
Total Prep & Cook Time: 5 hours 5 minutes
Total Macro Nutrients per Serving:
- 9 g Total Carbs
- 6 g Total Fats
- 2.5 g Total Protein
- 88 Calories

Fixings Needed:

- Olive oil (2 tbsp.)
- Tomato slices (6 cups)
- Grated parmesan (2 tbsp.)
- Salt (2 tsp.)
- Garlic powder (1 tsp.)
- Chopped basil (2 tbsp.)

Preparation Method:

1. Set the oven temperature at 350° Fahrenheit.
2. Slice the tomatoes and toss in with the oil.
3. Grate the parmesan in another container and add the garlic powder, salt, and basil.
4. Arrange the oiled tomatoes onto the baking sheet and sprinkle with the cheese mixture.
5. Bake until the edges begin charring.
6. Bake for 4-5 hours; checking every 30 minutes or so.

Tortilla Chips

Servings: 7
Total Prep & Cook Time: 25-30 minutes
Total Macro Nutrients per Serving:
- 4 g Net Carbs
- 18 g Total Fats
- 10 g Total Protein
- 220 Calories

Fixings Needed:

- Almond flour (2 cups)
- Egg (1 large)
- Garlic powder (.5 tsp.)
- Paprika (.25 tsp.)
- Chili powder (.5 tsp.)
- Cumin (.5 tsp.)
- Sea salt (.25 tsp.)
- Shredded mozzarella cheese (.5 cup)

Preparation Method:

1. Warm up the oven until it reaches 350° Fahrenheit.
2. Arrange parchment paper on a baking tin.
3. Combine the spices and flour in a mixing container. Mix in the egg using a hand mixer. It will form a crumbly dough.
4. Microwave the mozzarella until it's easy to stir or melt it in a double boiler on the stovetop.
5. Combine the fixings and knead. Arrange it between two pieces of parchment paper. Roll it out thinly using a rolling pin. Slice into triangles and place on the prepared baking tin.
6. Bake for 8-12 minutes. They'll be firm and golden.

Tasty Dips & Sauces for Snack time

Use these delicious dips to remain in ketosis. Just add your favorite veggies or a salty snack!

Avocado Ranch Dip

Servings: 4
Total Prep & Cook Time: 10-15 minutes
Total Macro Nutrients per Serving - .25 cup each:
- 1.4 g Net Carbs
- 17.8 g Total Fats
- 1.1 g Total Protein
- 171 Calories

Fixings Needed:

- Ripe avocado (1 medium)
- Plain non-fat yogurt (.33 cup)
- Coconut/avocado oil mayonnaise (.5 cup)
- Parsley (2 tbsp.)
- Dill (2 tbsp.)
- Worcestershire sauce - keto-friendly (1 tsp.)
- Clove of garlic (1)
- Salt (.25 tsp.)
- Onion powder (.25 tsp.)
- Black pepper (.25 tsp.)
- Smoked paprika (.5 tsp.)
- White vinegar (.5 tsp.)
- Also Needed: Food Processor

Preparation Method:

1. Freshly chop the dill and parsley. Mince the garlic clove.
2. Blend all of the ingredients until creamy smooth.
3. Taste and add spices to your liking.

4. Store in an airtight jar for a day or two at the most.

Blue Cheese Dip/Dressing

Servings: 4
Total Prep & Cook Time: 5 minutes
Total Macro Nutrients per Serving:
- 3.0 g Net Carbs
- 36 g Total Fats
- 9 g Total Protein
- 375 Calories

Fixings Needed:

- Blue cheese (5 oz.)
- Greek yogurt (.75 cup)
- Mayonnaise (.5 cup)
- Finely chopped fresh parsley (2 tbsp.)
- Salt and pepper (to your liking)
- Optional: Heavy whipping cream or water

Preparation Method:

1. Break the cheese apart and fold in the mayonnaise and yogurt. Mix well.
2. Let it sit for a two to three minutes. Sprinkle with the salt and pepper to taste.
3. If needed, dilute with the heavy cream a little bit of water.
4. Store in the fridge for 3 or 4 days.

Chili Dip

Servings: 32
Total Prep & Cook Time: 5 minutes
Total Macro Nutrients per Serving:
- 1.5 g Net Carbs
- 2.8 g Total Fats
- 1.5 g Total Protein
- 327 Calories

Fixings Needed:

- Chili without beans (15 oz.)
- Diced tomatoes with green chile pepper (10 oz.)
- Softened cream cheese (8 oz.)

Preparation Method:

1. Dice the tomatoes and add them to a microwave-safe mixing container. Mix in all of the fixings and microwave on high for one minute.
2. Stir and repeat the process until blended.

Creamy Avocado Cilantro Lime Dressing

Servings: 16
Total Prep & Cook Time: 10 minutes
Total Macro Nutrients - 1 cup Serving:
- 1.5 g Net Carbs
- 4.4 g Total Fats
- 0.5 g Total Protein
- 46 Calories

Fixings Needed:

- Peeled garlic clove (1)
- Avocado (1)
- Olive oil (3 tbsp.)
- Greek yogurt or low-fat sour cream (.25 cup)
- White vinegar or fresh lime juice (.25 cup)
- Black pepper (.25 tsp.)
- Kosher salt (.25 tsp.)
- Water (as needed)
- Also Recommended: Food processor or blender

Preparation Method:

1. Process all of the fixings with the blender until creamy.
2. Thin the dressing out with approximately 1/3 cup of water until it's the desired texture.
3. It will remain fresh for one to two weeks in an airtight serving pitcher.

Eggplant Dip

Servings: 6
Total Prep & Cook Time: 35 minutes
Total Macro Nutrients per Serving:
- 3.0 g Net Carbs
- 11 g Total Fats
- 2 g Total Protein
- 123 Calories

Fixings Needed:

- Eggplant (20 oz.)
- Sesame seeds (2 tbsp.)
- Ground cumin (.5 tsp.)
- Olive oil (.25 cup)
- Lemon juice (1 tbsp.)
- Salt and pepper (as desired)

Preparation Method:

1. Heat up the oven to 400° Fahrenheit. Use parchment paper to cover a baking tin.
2. Slice the eggplant lengthwise. Sprinkle with the salt and place the salty side upwards on the baking tin.
3. Bake until softened or for 30 minutes. Transfer to the counter to cool slightly. Peel away the skin and cube the eggplant into a bowl with the oil, pepper, lemon juice, and cumin. Blend

until it's a smooth consistency and season to taste. Set to the side.
4. Add a couple of tablespoons of sesame seeds to a hot and dry frying pan. Toast for a minute or two - stirring often.
5. Serve the dip in a bowl with the toasted seeds, sea salt and olive oil on top.

KETO SNACKS

5-Layer Mexican Dip Bowls You Can Eat with A Fork

Servings: 4
Total Prep & Cook Time: 35 minutes
Total Macro Nutrients per Serving:
- 11 g Net Carbs
- 82 g Total Fats
- 60 g Total Protein
- 1001 Calories

Fixings Needed:

- Avocados (2)
- Lime juice (1 tbsp.)
- Fresh cilantro (.25 cup)
- White onion (.25 cup)
- Tomato (.25 cup)
- Minced garlic (1 tsp.)
- Sea salt (.5 tsp.)

Preparation Method:

1. Do the prep. Peel and discard the avocado pit; chop. Squeeze the lime. Remove the seeds from the tomato and chop. Chop the garlic, onion, and cilantro.
2. Mash the avocado with the salt, garlic, tomato, onion, cilantro, and lime juice. Cover and place in the fridge.
3. Cook the beef in a skillet about 10 minutes. Discard the grease and add the water and seasonings.
4. Reduce the temperature setting. Continue to simmer for about ten more minutes. Portion into two bowls and top with the sour cream, guacamole, lettuce, and cheese.
5. Sprinkle with the cayenne as desired.

Guacamole

Servings: Makes 2 cups
Total Prep & Cook Time: 10-15 minutes
Total Macro Nutrients per Serving:
- 13 g Net Carbs
- 14 g Total Fats
- 3 g Total Protein
- 180 Calories

Fixings Needed:

- Whole Hass avocados (2)
- Red onion (.33 of 1 medium)
- Jalapeño (1 medium)
- Pre-made salsa (2 tbsp.)
- Fresh lime juice (1 tbsp.)
- Salt & Pepper (to taste)
- Fresh cilantro (.5 oz. or .5 of 1 bunch)

Preparation Method:

1. Slice both avocados into halves and remove the pits. Dice them while in the shell. Slice the limes in half. Dice the jalapeno and onion.
2. Combine all of the components of the recipe in a mixing bowl. Lightly mash the avocado and spritz with the lime juice.
3. Coarsely chop the half bunch of cilantros and toss into the guacamole.
4. Mix and serve as desired.

Keto-Friendly Mayonnaise

Servings: 1.25 cups total
Total Prep & Cook Time: 10-15 minutes
Total Macro Nutrients per Serving - 2 tablespoons each:
- -0- g Net Carbs
- 24 g Total Fats
- 1 g Total Protein
- 220 Calories

Fixings Needed:

- Egg (1)
- Freshly squeezed lemon juice (2 tbsp.)
- Salt (.5 tsp.)
- Dry mustard (1 tsp.)
- Avocado or olive oil (1.25 cups - divided)

Preparation Method:

1. Be sure the lemon juice and egg are room temperature before you start the prep.
2. Using a food processor, mix the mustard, salt, egg, juice, and 1/4 cup of the oil.
3. Process and slowly drizzle in the rest of the chosen oil. For the last two tablespoons - add quickly.

Olive Spread with Pecans

Servings: 12
Total Prep & Cook Time: 60 minutes
Total Macro Nutrients per Serving:
- 2.2 g Net Carbs
- 22 g Total Fats
- 2.5 g Total Protein
- 208 Calories

Fixings Needed:

- Green olives (5 oz.)
- Pecans (1 cup)
- Cream cheese (8 oz.)
- Keto-friendly mayonnaise (.5 cup)

Preparation Method:

1. Drain and slice the olives. Chop the pecans.
2. Combine each of the ingredients and stir well.
3. Place in the fridge for about an hour before serving.

Ranch Dip

Servings: 8
Total Prep & Cook Time: 15 minutes
Total Macro Nutrients per Serving:
- 1 g Net Carbs
- 26 g Total Fats
- 1 g Total Protein
- 241 Calories

Fixings Needed:

- Mayonnaise (1 cup)
- Ranch seasoning below (2 tbsp.)
- Sour cream (.5 cup)

Preparation Method:

1. Mix the components in a small dish.
2. Place it in the refrigerator for at least 15 minutes.
3. Store or serve when ready.

Ranch Seasoning

Servings: 1
Total Prep & Cook Time: 5 minutes
Total Macro Nutrients for The Entire Batch:
- 16 g Net Carbs
- 1 g Total Fats
- 5 g Total Protein
- 98 Calories

Fixings Needed:

- Dried tarragon or dried chives (2 tbsp.)
- Dried parsley (2 tbsp.)
- Garlic powder (1 tbsp.)
- Dried dill (2 tbsp.)
- Onion powder (1 tbsp.)
- Ground black pepper (.5 tbsp.)
- Sea salt (1 tbsp.)

Preparation Method:

1. Combine each of the fixings and add to a small jar.
2. Use for the ranch dressing to add flavor to your favorite snacks and other foods.

KETO SNACKS

Spicy Keto Pimento Cheese

Servings: 4
Total Prep & Cook Time: 15 minutes
Total Macro Nutrients per Serving:
- 1 g Net Carbs
- 24 g Total Fats
- 7 g Total Protein
- 246 Calories

Fixings Needed:

- Mayonnaise (5.33 tbsp.)
- Pimientos (4 tbsp.) or finely chopped pickled jalapeños
- Paprika powder or chili powder (1 tsp.)
- Dijon mustard (1 tbsp.)
- Cayenne pepper (1 pinch)
- Shredded cheddar cheese (4 oz.)
- For the Garnish: Chopped fresh chives or fresh parsley

Preparation Method:

1. Combine the fixings, omitting the chives.
2. Place in the refrigerator for at least one or two hours for best results.
3. Shape the mixture into balls and decorate with the chives.
4. Serve on top of some fried green tomatoes, with low-carb veggies, or as it is.
5. Store in the refrigerator for up to five days.

Pizza & Quiche Time

Bell Pepper Pizza

Servings: 4
Total Prep & Cook Time: 30 minutes
Total Macro Nutrients per Serving:
- 6.5 g Net Carbs
- 31.3 g Total Fats
- 22.3 g Total Protein
- 411.5 Calories

Fixings Needed For The Pizza Base:

- Mozzarella cheese (6 oz.)
- Fresh parmesan cheese (2 tbsp.)
- Cream cheese (2 tbsp.)
- Italian seasoning (1 tsp.)
- Psyllium husk (2 tbsp.)
- Large egg (1)
- Black pepper (.5 tsp.)
- Salt (.5 tsp.)

Fixings Needed For The Toppings:

- Shredded cheddar cheese (4 oz.)
- Marinara sauce (.25 cup)
- Medium tomato (1)
- Medium bell peppers (2-3)
- Freshly chopped basil (2 to 3 tbsp.)

Preparation Method:

1. Set the temperature in the oven to 400° Fahrenheit.
2. Melt the cheese in the microwave for 40 to 50 seconds or until pliable. Add the remainder of the pizza base fixings to the cheese and mix well.

3. Shape the dough to form two pizzas.
4. Bake for ten minutes. Remove and add the toppings.
5. Bake for another 8 to 10 minutes.
6. Cool slightly, slice, and serve.

KETO SNACKS

Cheese & Almond Pizza

Servings: 4
Total Prep & Cook Time: 20-25 minutes
Total Macro Nutrients per Serving:
- 5 g Net Carbs
- 45 g Total Fats
- 15 g Total Protein
- 450 Calories

Fixings Needed:

- Eggs (2)
- Alfredo sauce (.5 cup)
- Cheddar cheese (4 oz.)
- Butter (5 tbsp.)
- Almond meal (1 cup)
- Stevia (1.5 tsp.)
- Baking powder (1.5 tsp.)
- Garlic powder (.5 tsp.)
- Thyme (.25 tsp.)
- Oregano (.5 tsp.)

Preparation Method:

1. Spritz a pizza baking pan with cooking oil spray. Warm up the oven to 350° Fahrenheit.
2. Combine the dry fixings and mix well. Fold in the eggs. Melt the butter and add to the mixture.
3. Prepare the crust and spread it out evenly onto the pan. Cook the crust for 5 to 7 minutes.
4. Transfer it from the oven and add the alfredo sauce. Top it off with the cheese. Bake another 5 to 7 minutes.
5. Serve when golden.

Mini Crustless Quiche

Servings: 12
Total Prep & Cook Time: 35 minutes
Total Macro Nutrients per Serving:
- 2.9 g Net Carbs
- 11.2 g Total Fats
- 12 g Total Protein
- 159 Calories

Fixings Needed:

- Large eggs (15)
- Diced plum tomatoes (3)
- Shredded pepper jack cheese (.5 cup)
- Shredded mozzarella cheese (1 cup)
- Diced sweet onion (.33 cup)
- Sliced pickled jalapenos (.33 cup)
- Diced salami (1 cup)
- Heavy cream (.5 cup)
- Also Needed: Muffin tins - 11x15-inch

Preparation Method:

1. Warm up the temperature in the oven to 325° Fahrenheit.
2. Spritz the muffin tins lightly with a misting of cooking oil.
3. Whisk all of the fixings together and split the batter in the muffin tins.
4. Bake for 25 minutes. Cool and serve.

Pita Pizza

Servings: 2
Total Prep & Cook Time: 10-15 minutes
Total Macro Nutrients per Serving:
- 4 g Net Carbs
- 19 g Total Fats
- 13 g Total Protein
- 250 Calories

Fixings Needed:

- Marinara sauce (.5 cup)
- Low-carb pita (1)
- Cheddar cheese (2 oz.)
- Pepperoni (14 slices)
- Roasted red peppers (1 oz.)
- Spritz of olive oil

Preparation Method:

1. Program the oven setting to 450° Fahrenheit.
2. Slice the pita in half. Arrange it on a foil-lined baking tray and spritz with the oil. Toast for 1-2 minutes.
3. Empty the sauce over the prepared crust. Dust with the cheddar cheese and rest of the toppings.
4. Bake until the cheese melts or about five minutes.

Pizza Bites

Servings: 4
Total Prep & Cook Time: 10-15 minutes
Total Macro Nutrients per Serving:
- 2.8 g Net Carbs
- 7 g Total Fats
- 5 g Total Protein
- 94 Calories

Fixings Needed:

- Salami (4 slices)
- Marinara sauce (.25 cup)
- Shredded mozzarella (.25 cup)

Preparation Method:

1. Warm up the oven broiler using the high setting.
2. Add the salami on a baking sheet. Sprinkle with the sauce and cheese.
3. Prepare in the oven for five minutes. Drain the grease on a paper towel for 1 to 2 minutes. Serve.

Sausage & Salsa Quiche

Servings: 6
Total Prep & Cook Time: 60 minutes
Total Macro Nutrients per Serving:
- 3.5 g Net Carbs
- 35 g Total Fats
- 28 g Total Protein
- 443 Calories

Fixings Needed:

- Pork sausage (1 lb.)
- Eggs (3)
- Shredded cheese (8 oz.)
- Salsa (1 cup)
- Also Needed: 10-inch pie plate

Preparation Method:

1. Brown and break apart the sausage in a skillet.
2. When ready, drain away the grease and place the sausage in the pie plate. Top it off with about half of the cheese.
3. Whisk the eggs and mix in with the salsa. Scrape into the pan.
4. Bake until it's firm or about 30 minutes.
5. Sprinkle with the remainder of the cheese and bake until the cheese melts or another five minutes.
6. Wait 10 minutes before serving, or the quiche won't slice as it should. Slice into six sections and serve.

Smoked Sausage & Swiss Cheese Quiche

Servings: 6
Total Prep & Cook Time: 55-60 minutes
Total Macro Nutrients per Serving:
- 4 g Net Carbs
- 35 g Total Fats
- 20 g Total Protein
- 410 Calories

Fixings Needed:

- Eggs (6)
- Smoked sausage (.5 lb.)
- Shredded Swiss cheese (6 oz.)
- Salt (.5 tsp.)
- Minced chives (1 tsp.)
- Heavy cream (.75 cup)
- Also Needed: 9-10-inch pie plate

Preparation Method:

1. Warm up the oven temperature to 350° Fahrenheit. Lightly grease the pie plate.
2. Remove the casing from the smoked sausage. Slice lengthwise and into halves. Trim into half-moons.
3. Whisk the eggs and blend in the salt, chives, and cream.
4. Add the sausage and cheese layered in the bottom of the dish and pour in the egg ingredients.
5. Bake for 35 to 40 minutes.

Zucchini Pizza Bites

Servings: 4
Total Prep & Cook Time: 25 minutes
Total Macro Nutrients per Serving:
- 2 g Net Carbs
- 43 g Total Fats
- 26 g Total Protein
- 505 Calories

Fixings Needed:

- Large zucchini (3-4)
- Pizza sauce - no-sugar-added (.5 cup)
- Sliced pepperoni (12 oz.)
- Shredded mozzarella (1 cup)
- Freshly cracked black pepper & Salt (as desired)

Method of Preparation:

1. Heat up the oven to 350° Fahrenheit.
2. Slice the zucchini into 1/2-inch thick rounds. Arrange on a baking sheet and sprinkle with the salt and pepper.
3. Spoon equal portions of sauce on the rounds with a pinch or two of mozzarella cheese.
4. Garnish with the pepperoni and bake for 15-20 minutes.

Tacos & Wraps for Fun

Avocado Bacon Wrap

Servings: 1
Total Prep & Cook Time: 7 minutes
Total Macro Nutrients per Serving:
- 21 g Net Carbs
- 70 g Total Fats
- 37 g Total Protein
- 876 Calories

Fixings Needed:

- Keto-friendly mayonnaise (2 tbsp.)
- Roma tomato (.5 of 1 sliced)
- Sliced avocado (.5 of 1)
- Cooke bacon (2 strips)
- Lettuce leaves (2)
- Tortilla wrap (1)
- Salt and Pepper (to your liking)

Preparation Method:

1. Prepare each of the lettuce leaves with one tablespoon of mayo.
2. Add the bacon, sliced tomato, and avocado.
3. Dust with the pepper and salt. Wrap and serve.

Avocado & Salmon Omelet Wrap

Servings: 2
Total Prep & Cook Time: 30 minutes
Total Macro Nutrients per Serving:
- 6 g Net Carbs
- 67 g Total Fats
- 37 g Total Protein
- 765 Calories

Fixings Needed:

- Large eggs (3)
- Smoked salmon (1.8 oz.)
- Avocado (.5 of 1)
- Spring onion (1)
- Full-fat cream cheese (2.3 oz. or 2 tbsp.)
- Chives - freshly chopped (2 tbsp.)
- Butter or ghee (1 tbsp.)
- Pepper and salt (as desired)

Preparation Method:

1. Whisk the eggs and toss in a pinch of pepper and salt. Blend the chives and cream cheese well.
2. Prepare the salmon and avocado (peel, slice, or chop).
3. Combine the butter or ghee and the egg mixture in a frying pan. Continue cooking on low heat until done.
4. Arrange the omelet on a serving dish and spoon the mixture of cheese over it. Sprinkle the onion, prepared avocado, and salmon into the wrap.
5. Close and serve.

BLT Wrap

Servings: 1
Total Prep & Cook Time: 10 minutes
Total Macro Nutrients per Serving:
- 2 g Net Carbs
- 24 g Total Fats
- 8 g Total Protein
- 256 Calories

Fixings Needed:

- Crispy fried bacon slices (4)
- Romaine or Iceberg lettuce leaves (2)
- Chopped tomatoes (.25 cup)
- Mayonnaise (1 tbsp.)
- Pepper & Salt (to your liking)

Preparation Method:

1. Spread mayonnaise on one side of the lettuce.
2. Add the tomato and bacon. Garnish to your liking.
3. Roll it up and serve.

Chipotle Fish Tacos

Servings: 4
Total Prep & Cook Time: 20-25 minutes
Total Macro Nutrients per Serving:
- 7 g Net Carbs
- 20 g Total Fats
- 24 g Total Protein
- 300 Calories

Fixings Needed:
- Small yellow onion (.5 of 1)
- Jalapeno (1)
- Pressed garlic (2 cloves)
- Olive oil (2 tbsp.)
- Chipotle peppers in adobo sauce (4 oz.)
- Mayonnaise (2 tbsp.)
- Butter (2 tbsp.)
- Low-carb tortillas (4)
- Haddock fillets (1 lb. - 4 fillets)

Preparation Method:

1. Dice the onion and chop the jalapeno.
2. In a skillet, fry the onion for about five minutes using the medium-high heat setting.
3. Lower the heat setting to medium. Toss in the garlic and jalapeno. Stir for another 2 minutes.
4. Chop and add the chipotles, along with the adobo sauce.
5. Toss in the butter, mayonnaise, and fish into the pan and cook for about 8 minutes.
6. Make the Tacos: Fry to heat the tortilla for approximately 2 minutes for each side. Chill and shape them with the fish mixture.

Coleslaw Stuffed Wraps

Servings: 4
Total Prep & Cook Time: 30-35 minutes
Total Macro Nutrients per Serving:
- 3.1 g Net Carbs
- 50 g Total Fats
- 32.7 g Total Protein
- 609 Calories

Fixings Needed:

- Green onions (.5 cup)
- Red cabbage (3 cups)
- Apple cider vinegar (2 tsp.)
- Mayonnaise (.75 cup)
- Sea salt (.25 tsp.)

Fixings Needed For The Wraps & Other Fillings:

- Regular ground beef/turkey/chicken or pork (1 lb.)
- Collard leaves (16)
- Alfalfa sprouts (.33 cup - packed)
- Toothpicks

Preparation Method:

1. Fry the chosen meat in a skillet. Drain the grease and chill.
2. Trim away the stems from the collards and dice the onions. Thinly slice the cabbage. Rinse the collard leaves for the wrap and drain.
3. Add all of the fixings in a large mixing container – stirring well.
4. Add a spoonful of the coleslaw on the far edge of the first collard leaf (the side that hasn't been cut). Add the meat and the sprouts.
5. Roll and tuck the sides. Insert toothpicks at an angle to hold them together. Continue until all are finished.

Delicious Appetizers

Caprese Snacks

Servings: 4
Total Prep & Cook Time: 5 minutes
Total Macro Nutrients per Serving:
- 3.0 g Net Carbs
- 16 g Total Fats
- 13 g Total Protein
- 216 Calories

Fixings Needed:

- Cherry tomatoes (8)
- Mini mozzarella cheese balls (8 oz.)
- Green pesto (2 tbsp.)
- Pepper and salt (as desired)

Preparation Method:

1. Slice the mozzarella balls and tomatoes into halves.
2. Stir in the pesto and sprinkle with the pepper and salt to your liking.
3. Serve when you desire a healthy snack. You can also add some freshly chopped chives, parsley, or basil for a taste change.

KETO SNACKS

Salmon & Cream Cheese Bites

Servings: 36
Total Prep & Cook Time: 17-20 minutes
Total Macro Nutrients per Serving:
- 0.4 g Net Carbs
- 2.2 g Total Fats
- 1.9 g Total Protein
- 32 Calories

Fixings Needed:

- Cream or milk (1 cup)
- Eggs (6 medium)
- Salt (.5 tsp.)
- Dried dill (.5 tsp.)
- Cream cheese (.33 cup)
- Shredded cheese (.5 cup)
- Fresh/smoked salmon slices (1.8 oz.)
- Also Needed: Mini muffin trays or silicone molds

Preparation Method:

1. Whisk the salt, eggs, and milk in a large measuring cup.
2. Fold in the smoked salmon, shredded cheese, and diced cream cheese.
3. Pour into the molds and bake for 10-15 minutes at 350° Fahrenheit.
4. Cool before removing to serve.

CHAPTER 3

FAT BOMB FAVORITES

Cheesy Bacon Bombs

Servings: 20
Total Prep & Cook Time: 15-20 minutes
Total Macro Nutrients per Serving:
- 0.6 g Net Carbs
- 7.2 g Total Fats
- 5 g Total Protein
- 89 Calories

Fixings Needed:

- Bacon (10 slices)
- Mozzarella cheese (8 oz.)
- Melted butter (4 tbsp.)
- Almond flour (4 tbsp.)
- Psyllium husk powder (3 tbsp.)
- Large egg (1)
- Sea salt (.25 tsp.)
- Black pepper (.25 tsp.)
- Onion powder (.125 tsp.)

- Garlic powder (.125 tsp.)
- Lard or oil for frying (1 cup)

Preparation Method:

1. Warm up the oil/lard until it reaches 350° Fahrenheit in a pan or fryer.
2. Add about half the cheese into a microwavable dish and cook for 45 to 60 seconds until melted.
3. For the butter, microwave 15 to 20 seconds, and add to the cheese along with the egg.
4. Blend in the almond flour, psyllium husk, and spices. Arrange the dough on a silicone mat and roll out into a rectangular shape.
5. Add the remainder of cheese and fold to form a rectangle. Slice into 20 squares.
6. Wrap each segment with 1/2 slices of bacon and secure with a toothpick.
7. Cook each of the fat bombs (3-4 at a time) until crispy.
8. Remove from the oil, drain, and enjoy.

Pizza Fat Bombs

Servings: 6
Total Prep & Cook Time: 15-20 minutes
Total Macro Nutrients per Serving:
- 1.7 g Net Carbs
- 9.6 g Total Fats
- 2.26 g Total Protein
- 101.3 Calories

Fixings Needed:

- Cream cheese (4 oz.)
- Pepperoni slices (14)
- Pitted black olives (8)
- Freshly chopped basil (2 tbsp.)
- Sun-dried tomato pesto (2 tbsp.)
- Pepper & salt (as desired)

Preparation Method:

1. Dice the olives and pepperoni into small pieces and combine with the rest of the fixings and form into balls.
2. Sprinkle with the basil. Use a toothpick and decorate with 6 of the olives and pieces of pepperoni. For example, place the pepperoni on a dish with the bomb and add an olive on top.

Stuffed Pecan Fat Bombs

Servings: 1
Total Prep & Cook Time: 20 minutes
Total Macro Nutrients per Serving:
- 2 g Net Carbs
- 31 g Total Fats
- 11 g Total Protein
- 150 Calories

Fixings Needed:

- Pecan halves (4)
- Cream cheese (1 oz.)
- Coconut butter/unsalted butter (.5 tbsp.)
- Sea salt (1 pinch)
- Your favorite flavor mix – herb or veggie

Preparation Method:

1. Warm up the oven to 350° Fahrenheit. Once it's hot, toast the pecans for 8 to 10 minutes. Cool.
2. Let the cream cheese and butter soften. Add the mixture with your favorite flavored mix, veggie, or herbs. Mix until smooth.
3. Spread the tasty fixings between the two pecan halves.
4. Drizzle with some sea salt and serve.

Keto Sweet Bombs

Almond & Allspice Fat Bombs

Servings: 8
Total Prep & Cook Time: 10 minutes (+) 2 hrs. Chill time
Total Macro Nutrients per Serving:
- 2 g Net Carbs
- 22 g Total Fats
- 5 g Total Protein
- 214 Calories

Fixings Needed:

- Heavy cream (5 tbsp.)
- Almond butter (10 tbsp.)
- Coconut oil (4 tbsp.)
- Allspice (.25 tsp.)
- Cocoa powder (2 tsp.)
- Liquid stevia (6 drops)
- Chopped almonds (2 tbsp.)

Preparation Method:

1. Combine all of the fixings except for 3/4 of the almonds (adding last). Transfer the bombs into a mold or other storage container.
2. Freeze for approximately two hours. Top with the chopped almonds.
3. Remove and serve.

Almond Butter Fat Bombs

Servings: 8
Total Prep & Cook Time: 35 minutes
Total Macro Nutrients per Serving:
- 1.67 g Net Carbs
- 15 g Total Fats
- 1.5 g Total Protein
- 145 Calories

Fixings Needed:

- Almond butter (9.5 tbsp.)
- Melted coconut oil (.75 cup)
- Liquid stevia (3/8 tsp. or 60 drops)
- Melted salted butter (9 tbsp.)
- Cocoa (3 tbsp.)

Preparation Method:

1. Combine all of the ingredients listed until creamy smooth.
2. Pour into 24 mini muffin molds or use silicone candy molds.
3. Freeze for at least 30 minutes. Pop them out and eat any time.

Blackberry Coconut Fat Bombs

Servings: 16
Total Prep & Cook Time: 1 hour 30 minutes
Total Macro Nutrients per Serving:
- 3.0 g Net Carbs
- 18.7 g Total Fats
- 1.1 g Total Protein
- 170 Calories

Fixings Needed:

- Coconut oil (1 cup)
- Fresh or frozen blackberries (.5 cup)
- Coconut butter (1 cup)
- Vanilla extracts (.5 tsp.)
- Stevia drops (as desired)
- Lemon juice (1 tbsp.)
- Also Needed: 6x6 container

Fixings Needed:

1. Add the coconut oil, coconut butter, and frozen berries in a cooking pot using the medium heat setting. Line a baking pan with a sheet of parchment paper.
2. Use a small blender and add the mixture along with the rest of the components in the recipe. Spread it out on the prepared pan. Place the bombs in the fridge for about one hour.
3. *Note*: If you use fresh berries, you won't need to cook them with the butter and coconut oil (step 1).

Blueberry Frozen Fat Bombs

Servings: 24
Total Prep & Cook Time: 10 minutes (+) freeze time
Total Macro Nutrients per Serving:
- 1.02 g Net Carbs
- 13 g Total Fats
- .44 g Total Protein
- 116 Calories

Fixings Needed:

- Scant blueberries (1 cup)
- Butter (1 stick)
- Coconut oil (.75 cup)
- Softened cream cheese (4 oz.)
- Coconut cream (.25 cup)
- Sweetener of choice (to taste)

Preparation Method:

1. Arrange three to four berries in each mold cup.
2. Melt the butter with the coconut oil over the lowest stovetop heat setting. Cool slightly for approximately five minutes.
3. Combine all of the ingredients and whisk well. Slowly, add the sweetener.
4. Using a spouted pitcher, fill an ice tray with 24 bombs.
5. Pop them out and eat when hunger strikes.

Chocolate Fat Bombs

Servings: 14
Total Prep & Cook Time: 60-70 minutes
Total Macro Nutrients per Serving:
- 1.2 g Net Carbs
- 12.6 g Total Fats
- 1.4 g Total Protein
- 119 Calories

Fixings Needed:

- Tahini paste (1-2 tbsp.)
- Unsweetened cocoa powder (1 oz.)
- Walnut halves – for decoration (1 oz.)
- Coconut oil (4.5 oz.)
- Your favorite granulated sweetener (1 tbsp.)

Preparation Method:

1. Melt the coconut oil along with the rest of the fixings in a saucepan except for the walnuts.
2. Let the mixture cool slightly and pour into ice trays or candy molds.
3. Place in the fridge until mostly set. Add 1/2 of walnut on each one before serving.

Chocolate & PB Avocado Pudding Bomb

Servings: 1
Total Prep & Cook Time: 5 minutes
Total Macro Nutrients per Serving:
- 2 g Net Carbs
- 13 g Total Fats
- 2 g Total Protein
- 190 Calories

Fixings Needed:

- Ripe avocado (1)
- Natural peanut butter (1 tbsp.)
- Unsweetened almond milk (.5 cup)
- Vanilla (.5 tsp.)
- Steviva Blend (1-2 tbsp.)
- Cocoa powder (1 tbsp.)
- MCT Oil Powder - ex Perfect Keto (1 scoop)

Preparation Method:

1. Peel and chop the avocado. Combine with the rest of the fixings.
2. Add small portions of almond milk until it's like you like it.
3. For the sweetener; begin with 1 tablespoon and add slowly to taste.
4. Serve.

Chocolate & Peppermint Bombs

Servings: 6
Total Prep & Cook Time: 1.5 hours
Total Macro Nutrients per Serving:
- 1.1 g Net Carbs
- 21.1 g Total Fats
- 0.4 g Total Protein
- 188 Calories

Fixings Needed:

- Melted coconut oil (4.5 oz.)
- Granulated sweetener - your choice (1 tbsp.)
- Unsweetened coconut (2 tbsp.)
- Peppermint essence (.25 tsp.)

Preparation Method:

1. Combine the coconut oil, sweetener, and peppermint essence.
2. Pour about half of the bomb into six ice cube trays. Let them stay in the fridge for a white layer.
3. Use the remainder of the mixture to blend in with the cocoa powder.
4. Empty the chocolate mix on top of the trays.
5. Place it back into the fridge until firm. Pop it out and eat.

Cinnamon & Cardamom Fat Bombs

Servings: 10
Total Prep & Cook Time: 40 minutes
Total Macro Nutrients per Serving:
- 0.4 g Net Carbs
- 10 g Total Fats
- 0.4 g Total Protein
- 90 Calories

Fixings Needed:

- Unsalted butter (3 oz.)
- Unsweetened shredded coconut (.5 cup)
- Ground cinnamon (.25 tsp.)
- Ground cardamom - green (.25 tsp.)
- Vanilla extract (.5 tsp.)

Preparation Method:

1. Set the butter out ahead of time until it's room temperature
2. Carefully roast the shredded coconut until lightly browned and let it cool.
3. Combine about half of the coconut and butter together with the spices.
4. Form into ten portions and roll in the remainder of the coconut.
5. Place in the fridge or freezer until ready to eat.

Coconut & Cinnamon Bombs

Servings: 10
Total Prep & Cook Time: 2 hours
Total Macro Nutrients per Serving:
- 5.3 g Net Carbs
- 32 g Total Fats
- 3.3 g Total Protein
- 341 Calories

Fixings Needed:

- Vanilla extract (1 tsp.)
- Canned coconut milk - full-fat (1 cup)
- Coconut butter (1 cup)
- Shredded coconut (1 cup)
- Cinnamon (.5 tsp.)
- Nutmeg (.5 tsp.)
- Stevia powder extract (1 tsp.) Or 2-3 tbsp. raw honey (count the extra carbs)

Preparation Method:

1. Prepare a double boiler and add all ingredients (omitting the shredded coconut). Use medium heat until melted.
2. Let the mixture chill in the refrigerator for about 30 minutes.
3. Take the container out of the fridge and shape the mixture into ten balls. Roll them through the coconut pieces and refrigerate for a minimum of one hour.
4. Refrigerate until ready to eat.

Coconut Orange Creamsicle Fat Bombs

Servings: 10
Total Prep & Cook Time: 2-3 hours
Total Macro Nutrients per Serving:
- .95 g Net Carbs
- 19 g Total Fats
- 1.04 g Total Protein
- 177 Calories

Fixings Needed:

- Coconut oil (.5 cup)
- Heavy whipping cream (.5 cup)
- Cream cheese (4 oz.)
- Orange vanilla mio (1 tsp.)
- Liquid stevia (10 drops)
- Also Needed: Immersion blender & Silicone tray

Preparation Method:

1. Blend all of the ingredients together. If the mixture is too stiff, microwave it for a couple of seconds.
2. Spread the fixings into the tray and freeze for about two to three hours.
3. Once it's hardened, transfer to a container and store in the freezer until desired.

KETO SNACKS

Coffee Fat Bombs

Servings: 15
Total Prep & Cook Time: 2 hours 15 minutes
Total Macro Nutrients per Serving:
- -0- g Net Carbs
- 4 g Total Fats
- -0- g Total Protein
- 45 Calories

Fixings Needed:

- Cream cheese - room temperature (4.4 oz.)
- Powdered xylitol (2 tbsp.)
- Instant coffee (1 tbsp.)
- Unsweetened cocoa powder (1 tbsp.)
- Room-temperature butter (1 tbsp.)
- Coconut oil (1 tbsp.)

Preparation Method:

1. With a blender/food processor, blitz the xylitol and coffee into a fine powder. Add the hot water to form a pasty mix.
2. Blend in the cream cheese, butter, cocoa powder, and coconut oil.
3. Add to ice cube trays and freeze a minimum of one to two hours.
4. Use a zipper-type baggie to keep them fresh in the freezer.

Dark Chocolate Fat Bombs

Servings: 12
Total Prep & Cook Time: 1 hour 20 minutes
Total Macro Nutrients per Serving:
- 5.6 g Net Carbs
- 10.5 g Total Fats
- 4 g Total Protein
- 96 Calories

Fixings Needed:

- Stevia extract (1 tsp.)
- Butter/coconut oil (.5 cup)
- Almond butter (.5 cup)
- Dark chocolate – 85% or higher (3 oz.)
- Sea salt (.25 tsp.)

Preparation Method:

1. Mix all of the components in the recipe until smooth using a double boiler.
2. Empty the mixture into 12 ice trays. Freeze for at least one hour.
3. Serve when desired.

Neapolitan Fat Bombs

Servings: 24
Total Prep & Cook Time: 2.5 hours
Total Macro Nutrients per Serving:
- 0.66 g Net Carbs
- 10.99 g Total Fats
- 0.51 g Total Protein
- 102.7 Calories

Fixings Needed:

- Butter (.5 cup)
- Coconut oil (.5 cup)
- Sour cream (.5 cup)
- Cream cheese (.5 cup)
- Erythritol (2 tbsp.)
- Liquid stevia (25 drops)
- Cocoa powder (2 tbsp.)
- Strawberries (2 medium)
- Vanilla extract (1 tsp.)
- Also Needed: Immersion blender & Fat bomb mold

Preparation Method:

1. Combine each of the fixings except for the strawberries, cocoa, and vanilla. Mix with the immersion blender.
2. Divide the mixture into three dishes; adding the vanilla in one, cocoa in one, and the berries in the last dish.
3. Pour the chocolate powder into the mold and freeze for about 30 minutes. Continue the process with the vanilla layer (30 min.) and the strawberry layer.
4. Freeze together for at least one hour.

No-Bake Lemon Cheesecake Fat Bombs

Servings: 12
Total Prep & Cook Time: 10 minutes
Total Macro Nutrients per Serving:
- 1.0 g Net Carbs
- 9 g Total Fats
- 1.0 g Total Protein
- 80 Calories

Fixings Needed:

- Coconut oil (.25 cup)
- Unsalted butter (.25 cup)
- Cream cheese (4 oz.)
- Favorite natural sweetener (2 tbsp.)
- Fresh lemon juice (1 oz.)
- Lemon zest (1 lemon) optional
- Blueberries or your favorite berries (12)
- Also Needed: Silicone molds - mini-muffin liners - ice cube trays or onto wax paper

Preparation Method:

1. Use a hand mixer to blend the butter, coconut oil, cream cheese, and sweetener together until creamy smooth.
2. Grate and add the lemon zest and juice.
3. Toss a blueberry into each of the bombs and freeze until firm.
4. Pop each one out the molds and keep frozen in an airtight container until you need them.

Pistachio & Almond Fat Bombs

Servings: 36
Total Prep & Cook Time: 20 minutes (+) 4 hours chill time
Total Macro Nutrients per Serving:
- 3.1 g Net Carbs
- 17.4 g Total Fats
- 2.2 g Total Protein
- 170 Calories

Fixings Needed:

- Full-fat coconut milk (.5 cup)
- Roasted almond butter (1 cup)
- Firm coconut oil (1 cup)
- Creamy coconut butter (1 cup)
- Chai spice (2 tsp.)
- Ghee (.25 cup)
- Himalayan salt (.25 tsp.)
- Pure almond extract (.25 tsp.)
- Pure vanilla extract (1 tbsp.)
- Cacao butter - melted (.5 cup)
- Raw shelled pistachios (.25 tsp.)
- Also Needed: 9-inch square baking pan

Preparation Method:

1. Chill the coconut milk overnight.
2. Grease the pan and line it with parchment paper.
3. Melt the butter in a saucepan or microwave and set aside.
4. Add everything except the pistachios and cacao butter in a large bowl. Use the slow speeds and increase using a hand mixer until it is airy and light.
5. Empty the melted cacao into the almond mix and continue mixing until it is well incorporated. Add it to the prepared pan and sprinkle with the chopped pistachios.

6. Refrigerate for at least 4 hours. It's much better if chilled overnight.
7. Cut into 36 squares.

CHAPTER 4

HIGH-FAT KETO SNACKS FOR VEGETARIANS

First, you should recognize there are three types of vegetarians:

- Vegans avoid seafood, poultry, dairy, eggs, meat, and other animal products, including honey, in most cases.

- Lacto vegetarians eat dairy but avoid eggs, seafood, poultry, and meat. People in India who are vegetarians mainly follow this way of eating.

- Lacto-ovo vegetarians eat dairy and eggs but avoid seafood, poultry, and meat. This is the most common form of vegetarianism in the United States, Europe, and other western countries.

You should also include protein, restrict carbs, use healthy cooking oils and salad dressings, and have at least one to three servings of vegetables daily. You still want to season your food with spices and herbs as you would on the regular ketogenic diet plan.

These are just several examples of snacks and foods you can enjoy as a vegetarian to receive your proteins:

KETO SNACKS

- Cottage cheese: 20 grams of protein and 6 grams of carbs per 6 ounces (170 grams)

- Parmesan and Romano cheese: 9–10 grams of protein and 1 gram carb per ounce (28 grams)

- Hard and semi-hard cheese (cheddar, gouda, provolone, Swiss, etc.): 7–8 grams of protein and 0.5–1.5 grams of carbs per ounce (28 grams)

- Soft cheese (Brie, feta, blue cheese, etc.): 4–6 grams of protein and 0–1 of gram carb per ounce (28 grams)

- Peanut or almond butter: 7–8 grams of protein and 4 grams of net carbs per 2 tablespoons (32 grams)

Vegetarian-Friendly Ketogenic Beverages

Coffee & Cream

Servings: 1
Total Prep & Cook Time: 5 minutes
Total Macro Nutrients per Serving:
- 2 g Net Carbs
- 22 g Total Fats
- 2 g Total Protein
- 206 Calories

Fixings Needed:

- Brewed coffee (.75 cup)
- Heavy whipping cream (4 tbsp.)

Preparation Method:

1. Prepare your coffee to your liking.
2. Add the cream in a saucepan and simmer until it's frothy.
3. Pour the cream into the cup and gently stir.
4. Serve with a slice of cheese or a handful of nuts for a quick 'pick-me-up.'

Hot Chocolate

Servings: 1
Total Prep & Cook Time: 5 minutes
Total Macro Nutrients per Serving:
- 1 g Net Carbs
- 23 g Total Fats
- 1 g Total Protein
- 216 Calories

Fixings Needed:

- Cocoa powder (1 tbsp.)
- Unsalted butter (1 oz.)
- Vanilla extract (.25 tsp.)
- Boiling water (1 cup)
- Powdered erythritol - optional (1 tsp.)
- Also Needed: Immersion blender

Preparation Method:

1. Add each of the ingredients into a tall container to prepare using the blender. Mix for about 15 to 20 seconds until the foam is no longer on the top.
2. Pour the cocoa into the cups and serve.

Pumpkin Spice Latte

Servings: 1
Total Prep & Cook Time: 5 minutes
Total Macro Nutrients per Serving:
- 1 g Net Carbs
- 23 g Total Fats
- 0.5 g Total Protein
- 216 Calories

Fixings Needed:

- Boiling water (1 cup)
- Pumpkin pie spice or cinnamon (1 tsp.)
- Unsalted butter (1 oz.)
- Instant coffee powder (1-2 tsp)
- Also Needed: Immersion Blender

Preparation Method:

1. Combine the instant coffee, spices, and butter in a mixing dish.
2. Add the water and blend for 20 to 30 seconds until foamy.
3. Pour into the cup and sprinkle with the spice.
4. Serve with a dollop of whipped cream on top to your liking.

Vanilla Coffee & Whipped Cream

Servings: 1
Total Prep & Cook Time: 5 minutes
Total Macro Nutrients per Serving:
- 2 g Net Carbs
- 21 g Total Fats
- 2 g Total Protein
- 206 Calories

Fixings Needed:

- Heavy whipping cream (.25 cup)
- Coffee (1 cup prepared)
- Vanilla extract (.25 tsp.)
- Optional Garnish: Cocoa powder or Ground cinnamon

Preparation Method:

1. Prepare your coffee as you normally do without the extras.
2. Whip the cream with the vanilla to form soft peaks.
3. Pour the coffee into a large mug with a dollop of cream.
4. Sprinkle with a dusting of cinnamon or cocoa powder to your liking.
5. Serve and enjoy with a portion of nuts for a healthy snack.

Delicious Vegetarian Snacks

Cheese Puffs

Servings: 3
Total Prep & Cook Time: 5 minutes
Total Macro Nutrients per Serving:
- 0.2 g Net Carbs
- 14 g Total Fats
- 10 g Total Protein
- 167 Calories

Fixings Needed:

- Brie Cheese (5.33 oz.)

Preparation Method:

1. Slice the cheese into cubes about .5 inches thick. Remove the white edge.
2. Arrange a few slices on a parchment-lined platter.
3. Place in the microwave for one to two minutes using the full-power setting.
4. Watch carefully, making a few at a time.
5. Cool before serving and spice to your liking.

Cheese Roll-Ups

Servings: 4
Total Prep & Cook Time: 5 minutes
Total Macro Nutrients per Serving:
- 2 g Net Carbs
- 31 g Total Fats
- 13 g Total Protein
- 335 Calories

Fixings Needed:

- Butter (2 oz.)
- Cheddar/Provolone/Edam cheese slices (8 oz.)

Preparation Method:

1. Arrange the slices on a cutting board.
2. Thinly slice the butter and place in each of the slices.
3. Roll them up and sprinkle with your favorite spices for a quick snack.

Keto Bread Twists

Servings: 10
Total Prep & Cook Time: 30 minutes
Total Macro Nutrients per Serving:
- 1 g Net Carbs
- 18 g Total Fats
- 7 g Total Protein
- 204 Calories

Fixings Needed:

- Almond flour (.5 cup)
- Coconut flour (4 tbsp.)
- Salt (.5 tsp.)
- Baking powder (1 tsp.)
- Shredded cheese - preferably mozzarella (1.5 cups)
- Butter (2.33 oz.)
- Egg (2 - Use 1 for brushing the tops)
- Green pesto (2 oz.)

Preparation Method:

1. Warm up the oven to reach 350° Fahrenheit. Line a baking sheet with a layer of parchment paper.
2. Combine all the dry fixings.
3. Use the low heat setting to melt the butter and cheese together. Stir until smooth and add the egg. Stir well.
4. Combine all of the fixings to make the dough.
5. Roll out the dough between two layers of parchment paper until it is about one inch thick. Remove the top sheet.
6. Spread the pesto on top of the dough and slice into one-inch strips.
7. Twist the dough and arrange on the baking tin. Brush the twists with the second egg (whisked).
8. Bake until golden brown or about 15 to 20 minutes.

Keto Spicy Roasted Nuts

Servings: 6
Total Prep & Cook Time: 15 minutes
Total Macro Nutrients per Serving:
- 2 g Net Carbs
- 29 g Total Fats
- 4 g Total Protein
- 281 Calories

Fixings Needed:

- Olive/coconut oil (1 tbsp.)
- Salt (1 tsp.)
- Walnuts/almonds/pecans (8 oz.)
- Ground cumin (1 tsp.)
- Chili/paprika powder (1 tsp.)

Preparation Method:

1. Combine each of the components in a skillet.
2. Prepare using the medium temperature setting until warm.
3. Cool as a delicious snack with your favorite beverage.
4. Store at room temperature in a closed container.

Roasted Almonds

Servings: 4
Total Prep & Cook Time: 10 minutes
Total Macro Nutrients per Serving:
- 11.5 g Net Carbs
- 31.1 g Total Fats
- 10.2 g Total Protein
- 342 Calories

Fixings Needed:

- Blanched almonds (2 cups)
- Rosemary (2 tbsp.)
- Salt (1 tsp.)
- Paprika (1 tsp.)
- Olive oil (2 tbsp.)

Preparation Method:

1. Toast the almonds in a pan using the med-high temperature setting.
2. Lower to med-low and stir in the rosemary, paprika, and salt.
3. Continue cooking for about 3 more minutes before serving.

Slow-Roasted Cashews

Servings: 4
Total Prep & Cook Time: 3 hours 5 minutes (+) soak time
Total Macro Nutrients per Serving:
- 13.9 g Net Carbs
- 15.9 g Total Fats
- 5.4 g Total Protein
- 205 Calories

Fixings Needed:

- Cinnamon (2 tbsp.)
- Water (1 cup)
- Cashews (1 cup)

Preparation Method:

1. Pour the cashews and water into a container to soak overnight.
2. Drain and allow to dry on a paper towel.
3. Warm up the oven to 200° Fahrenheit.
4. Toss the cashews on a baking tray and sprinkle with the cinnamon.
5. Roast for 3 hours. Cool before serving.

Sun-Dried Tomato Pesto Mug Cake

Servings: 1
Total Prep & Cook Time: 4-5 minutes
Total Macro Nutrients per Serving:
- 5.32 g Net Carbs
- 40.45 g Total Fats
- 12.34 g Total Protein
- 429 Calories

Fixings Needed For The Base:

- Butter (2 tbsp.)
- Large egg (1)
- Baking powder (.5 tsp.)
- Almond flour (2 tbsp.)

Fixings Needed For Seasoning:

- Sun-dried tomato pesto (5 tsp.)
- Salt (1 pinch)
- Almond flour (1 tbsp.)

Preparation Method:

1. Combine each of the ingredients together in a microwavable dish.
2. Cook (power level 10) for 75 seconds using the high setting.
3. Place the cup upside down on a plate and the cake should slide out.
4. Add the tomato pesto to serve.

Sweet Vegetarian Snacks

Chia Raspberry Pudding

Servings: 2
Total Prep & Cook Time: 3 hours 10 minutes
Total Macro Nutrients per Serving:
- 22.3 g Net Carbs
- 38.8 g Total Fats
- 9.1 g Total Protein
- 408 Calories

Fixings Needed:

- Chia seeds (4 tbsp.)
- Raspberries (.5 cup)
- Coconut milk (1 cup)
- Also Needed: 2 mason jars

Preparation Method:

1. Pour the milk and raspberries into a blender.
2. Pulse until smooth. Pour into the jars.
3. Fold in the chia seeds and stir.
4. Secure the lid and shake.
5. Store in the fridge for at least three hours before enjoying.

Choco Mug Brownie

Servings: 1
Total Prep & Cook Time: 10 minutes
Total Macro Nutrients per Serving:
- 9.5 g Net Carbs
- 15.8 g Total Fats
- 12.4 g Total Protein
- 207 Calories

Fixings Needed:

- Chocolate protein powder (1 scoop)
- Cocoa powder (1 tbsp.)
- Baking powder (.5 tsp.)
- Almond milk (.25 cup)

Preparation Method:

1. Prepare a mug using the protein powder, cocoa, and baking powder.
2. Pour the milk into the mug and stir.
3. Microwave for about 30 seconds and serve.

Chocolate & Hazelnut Spread

Servings: 6
Total Prep & Cook Time: 10 minutes
Total Macro Nutrients per Serving:
- 2 g Net Carbs
- 28 g Total Fats
- 4 g Total Protein
- 271 Calories

Fixings Needed:

- Coconut oil (.25 cup)
- Hazelnuts (5 oz.)
- Unsalted butter (1 oz.)
- Vanilla extract (1 tsp.)
- Cocoa powder (2 tbsp.)
- Optional: Erythritol (1 tsp.)

Preparation Method:

1. Prepare a skillet on the stovetop until hot. Toss in the hazelnuts and roast until golden. Let them cool slightly.
2. Arrange the nuts in a kitchen towel to rub away some of the shells. (If they're stuck, that is okay.)
3. Place all of the ingredients into a blender/processor. Mix well until you reach the desired consistency.
4. Tip: Serve as a delicious and healthy dip for fresh strawberries or as a spread for rolls, waffles, or pancakes.

Cinnamon Coconut Chips

Servings: 2
Total Prep & Cook Time: 10 minutes
Total Macro Nutrients per Serving:
- 7.8 g Net Carbs
- 21 g Total Fats
- 1.9 g Total Protein
- 228 Calories

Fixings Needed:

- Unsweetened coconut chips (1 cup)
- Cinnamon (.25 tsp.)
- Sea salt (.25 tsp.)

Preparation Method:

1. Whisk the salt and cinnamon together.
2. Use the medium heat setting to warm a skillet (2 min.).
3. Stir in the chips and stir until lightly browned.
4. Toss in with the salt and cinnamon mixture before serving.

Coffee Cake

Servings: 8
Total Prep & Cook Time: 1.75 hours
Total Macro Nutrients per Serving:
- 4.2 g Net Carbs
- 28 g Total Fats
- 13 g Total Protein
- 321 Calories

Fixings Needed For The Base:

- Eggs (6 separated)
- Cream cheese (6 oz.)
- Erythritol (.25 cup)
- Liquid stevia (.25 tsp.)
- Unflavored protein powder (.25 cup)
- Vanilla extract (2 tsp.)
- Cream of tartar (.25 tsp.)

Fixings Needed For The Filling:

- Almond flour (1.5 cups)
- Cinnamon (1 tbsp.)
- Butter (.5 stick)
- Maple Syrup Substitute (.25 cup)
- Erythritol (.25 cup)
- Also Needed: Dark metal cake pan

Preparation Method:

1. Warm up the oven to 325° Fahrenheit.
2. Separate eggs from egg whites and add the erythritol with egg yolks.
3. Combine and whisk all other ingredients except for cream of tartar and egg whites.
4. Whip the egg whites and cream of tartar until stiff peaks form. Gently fold half of the egg white mixture into the yolks and then the other half.
5. Mix all of the filling fixings to form the dough.
6. Pour the base batter into the pan and top with half of the cinnamon filling. Push it down some if it does not collapse on its own.
7. Bake for 20 minutes and then top the cake off with the rest of the filling dough.
8. Bake for another 20 to 30 minutes. It's done when a toothpick comes out clean. Cool for 10 to 20 minutes before removing from the pan to serve.

Crunchy Berry Mousse

Servings: 8
Total Prep & Cook Time: 10 minutes (+) 4 hours chill time
Total Macro Nutrients per Serving:
- 3.0 g Net Carbs
- 27 g Total Fats
- 3 g Total Protein
- 260 Calories

Fixings Needed:

- Heavy whipping cream (2 cups)
- Vanilla extract (.25 tsp.)
- Lemon (.5 of 1 - zested)
- Chopped pecans (2 oz.)
- Fresh raspberries/blueberries/strawberries (3 oz.)

Preparation Method:

1. Use a hand mixer to whip the cream until it forms soft peaks. Then, add the vanilla and lemon zest when formed.
2. Fold in the nuts and berries. Stir.
3. Cover with a layer of plastic wrap.
4. For a firmer mousse, store in the fridge for about four hours.
5. You can enjoy it when freshly prepared if you like it less firm.

Keto Brunch Brownies

Servings: 6
Total Prep & Cook Time: 20-22 minutes
Total Macro Nutrients per Serving:
- 4.37 g Net Carbs
- 14.09 g Total Fats
- 6.98 g Total Protein
- 193 Calories

Fixings Needed:

- Golden flaxseed meal (1 cup)
- Cocoa powder (.25 cup)
- Cinnamon (1 tbsp.)
- Baking powder (.5 tbsp.)
- Salt (.5 tsp.)
- Egg (1 large)
- Coconut oil (2 tbsp.)
- Sugar-free caramel syrup (.25 cup)
- Pumpkin puree (.5 cup)
- Vanilla extract (1 tsp.)
- Apple cider vinegar (1 tsp.)
- Slivered almonds (.25 cup)

Preparation Method:

1. Warm up the oven to 350° Fahrenheit. Mix each of the fixings until well combined.
2. Line a muffin tin with 6 paper liners. Spoon about ¼ of a cup of the batter into each muffin liner.
3. Sprinkle the slivered almonds over the top of each muffin and press gently.
4. Bake for about 15 minutes.

Peanut Butter Fudge

Servings: 20
Total Prep & Cook Time: 1 hour 15 minutes
Total Macro Nutrients per Serving:
- 6.2 g Net Carbs
- 11.3 g Total Fats
- 4.3 g Total Protein
- 135 Calories

Fixings Needed:

- Coconut oil (3 tbsp.)
- Smooth peanut butter - keto-friendly (12 oz.)
- Coconut cream (4 tbsp.)
- Maple syrup (4 tbsp.)
- Salt (1 pinch)

Preparation Method:

1. Prepare a baking sheet with a layer of parchment paper.
2. Melt the syrup and coconut oil using the medium heat setting on the stovetop.
3. Stir in the salt, coconut cream, and peanut butter. Pour the mixture into the prepared dish and chill in the fridge for at least one hour.
4. Slice into pieces and store or serve.

Pistachio Ice Cream

Servings: 3
Total Prep & Cook Time: 23 minutes
Total Macro Nutrients per Serving:
- 15.8 g Net Carbs
- 43.8 g Total Fats
- 6.3 g Total Protein
- 457 Calories

Fixings Needed:

- Egg yolks (2)
- Coconut milk (1.75 cups)
- Honey (1 tbsp.)
- Oil (1 tbsp.)
- Chopped pistachio nuts (5 tbsp.)
- Vanilla (1 tsp.)

Preparation Method:

1. Whisk the milk, oil, eggs, honey, and salt in a mixing container. Place in the fridge for about one hour.
2. Roast the chopped pistachios using the medium heat setting.
3. Prepare the ice cream maker and add the mixture into the bowl.
4. About halfway through the cycle, add the pistachio nuts.
5. Serve any time for a delicious snack.

White Chocolate Fat Bomb - Vegetarian

Servings: 8
Total Prep & Cook Time: 15 minutes (+) 1-hour chill time
Total Macro Nutrients per Serving:
- 0.3 g Net Carbs
- 20.2 g Total Fats
- 0.9 g Total Protein
- 265 Calories

Fixings Needed:

- Erythritol (4 tbsp. powdered)
- Butter (4 tbsp.)
- Coconut oil (4 tbsp.)
- Cocoa butter (4 oz.)
- Chopped walnuts (.5 cup)
- Vanilla extract (.5 tsp.)
- Salt (.25 tsp)

Preparation Method:

1. Prepare a pan using the medium-high temperature setting on the stovetop. Add the butter, coconut oil, and cocoa butter.
2. Once it's melted, add the walnuts, salt, stevia, vanilla extract, and erythritol. Mix well.
3. Pour into the silicone mold and place in the fridge for one hour before serving.

CHAPTER 5

DELICIOUS SMOOTHIES & FROZEN TREATS FOR SNACKS

Almond & Blueberry Smoothie

Servings: 2
Total Prep & Cook Time: 5 minutes
Total Macro Nutrients per Serving:
- 6 g Net Carbs
- 25 g Total Fats
- 15 g Total Protein
- 302 Calories

Fixings Needed:

- Unsweetened almond milk (16 oz.)
- Heavy cream (4 oz.)
- Stevia (to taste)
- Whey vanilla isolate powder (1 scoop)
- Frozen unsweetened blueberries (.25 cup)

Preparation Method:

KETO SNACKS

1. Pour the milk along with the rest of the ingredients into a blender.
2. Mix until smooth.
3. Serve it up in a couple of chilled glasses.

Almond Strawberry Smoothie

Servings: 2
Total Prep & Cook Time: 5-6 minutes
Total Macro Nutrients per Serving:
- 7 g Net Carbs
- 25 g Total Fats
- 15 g Total Protein
- 304 Calories

Fixings Needed:

- Heavy cream (.5 cup)
- Unsweetened almond milk (16 oz.)
- Stevia (to taste)
- Frozen unsweetened strawberries (.25 cup)
- Whey vanilla isolate powder (2 tbsp.)

Preparation Method:

1. Toss or pour each of the ingredients into a blender.
2. Puree until smooth.
3. Add a small amount of water to thin the smoothie if needed.

Avocado Mint Green Smoothie

Servings: 1
Total Prep & Cook Time: 4-5 minutes
Total Macro Nutrients per Serving:
- 5 g Net Carbs
- 23 g Total Fats
- 1 g Total Protein
- 221 Calories

Fixings Needed:

- Almond milk (.5 cup)
- Full-fat coconut milk (.75 cup)
- Avocado (3-4 oz. or .5 of 1)
- Cilantro (3 sprigs)
- Mint leaves (5-6 large)
- Vanilla extract (.25 tsp.)
- Lime juice (1 squeeze)
- Sweetener of your choice (as desired)
- Crushed ice (1.5 cups)

Preparation Method:

1. Measure each of the ingredients into the blender.
2. Mix well using the low-speed setting until pureed.
3. Toss in the ice and mix. Serve in a cold mug.

Avocado Raspberry Smoothie

Servings: 2
Total Prep & Cook Time: 4-5 minutes
Total Macro Nutrients per Serving:
- 4 g Net Carbs
- 20 g Total Fats
- 2.5 g Total Protein
- 227 Calories

Fixings Needed:

- Ripe avocado (1)
- Lemon juice (3 tbsp.)
- Water (1.33 cups)
- Unsweetened - frozen raspberries/or choice of berries (.5 cup)
- Your choice sugar equivalent (1 tbsp. (+) 1 tsp.)

Preparation Method:

1. Mix all of the ingredients in a blender until smooth.
2. Pour the smoothie into two chilled glasses and serve.

Blackberry Cheesecake Smoothie

Servings: 1
Total Prep & Cook Time: 4-5 minutes
Total Macro Nutrients per Serving:
- 6.7 g Net Carbs
- 53 g Total Fats
- 6.4 g Total Protein
- 515 Calories

Fixings Needed:

- Extra-virgin coconut oil (1 tbsp.)
- Fresh/frozen blackberries (.5 cup)
- Water (.5 cup)
- Coconut milk/heavy whipping cream (.25 cup)
- Full-fat cream cheese or creamed coconut milk (.25 cup)
- Sugar-free vanilla extract (.5 tsp.)
- Liquid stevia (3 to 5 drops as desired)

Preparation Method:

1. Arrange all of the fixings in the blender.
2. Pulse until the mixture is smooth and frothy.
3. Add a few ice cubes and enjoy it in a chilled glass.

Blackcurrant Smoothie

Servings: 1
Total Prep & Cook Time: 10 minutes
Total Macro Nutrients per Serving:
- 8.7 g Net Carbs
- 17.3 g Total Fats
- 5.1 g Total Protein
- 228 Calories

Fixings Needed:

- Water (.5 cup)
- Frozen or fresh blackcurrants (2.1 oz.)
- Frozen or fresh strawberries (.25 cup or 2-3 berries)
- Heavy whipping cream/coconut milk (.25 cup)
- Chia seeds - powdered or whole (2 tbsp.)
- Sugar-free vanilla extract/1 vanilla bean (.5 tsp.)
- Stevia liquid - optional (4-7 drops)

Preparation Method:

1. Toss all of the components of the smoothie into a blender.
2. Pulse until creamy. Let it rest for about 5 minutes for the flavors to mix.
3. Note: Add ice either before or after mixing.

Blueberry Smoothie

Servings: 1
Total Prep & Cook Time: 5 minutes
Total Macro Nutrients per Serving:
- 3.0 g Net Carbs
- 21 g Total Fats
- 31 g Total Protein
- 343 Calories

Fixings Needed:

- Coconut milk (1 cup)
- Blueberries (.25 cup)
- Vanilla essence (1 tsp.)
- MCT oil (1 tsp.)
- Optional: Whey protein powder (1 scoop)

Preparation Method:

1. Toss all of the fixings into the blender.
2. Toss in a few ice cubes.
3. Blend until smooth.

Blueberry - Banana Bread Smoothie

Servings: 2
Total Prep & Cook Time: 5 minutes
Total Macro Nutrients per Serving:
- 4.7 g Net Carbs
- 23.3 g Total Fats
- 3.1 g Total Protein
- 270 Calories

Fixings Needed:

- Chia seeds (1 tbsp.)
- Golden flaxseed meal (3 tbsp.)
- Vanilla unsweetened coconut milk (2 cups)
- Blueberries (.25 cup)
- Liquid stevia (10 drops)
- MCT oil (2 tbsp.)
- Xanthan gum (.25 tsp.)
- Banana extract (1.5 tsp.)
- Ice cubes (2-3)

Preparation Method:

1. Combine all of the ingredients into a blender.
2. Wait a few minutes for the seeds and flax to absorb some of the liquid.
3. Pulse for one or two minutes until well combined.
4. Add the ice to your preference.

Blueberry - Chia & Coconut Smoothie

Servings: 3
Total Prep & Cook Time: 5-8 minutes
Total Macro Nutrients per Serving:
- 11.3 g Net Carbs
- 21.1 g Total Fats
- 6.2 g Total Protein
- 249 Calories

Fixings Needed:

- Coconut (.5 cup)
- Unsweetened cashew or almond milk (1 cup)
- Ground chia seed (2 tbsp.)
- Frozen blueberries (1 cup)
- Full-fat Greek yogurt or almond milk (1 cup)
- Sweetener of choice (equal to 2 tbsp. sugar)
- Coconut oil (2 tbsp.)
- Optional: Cubes of ice (2-3)

Preparation Method:

1. Carefully measure the ingredients and put them into your blender.
2. Mix until creamy smooth. Serve in three chilled glasses.

Blueberry Yogurt Smoothie

Servings: 2
Total Prep & Cook Time: 5 minutes
Total Macro Nutrients per Serving:
- 2 g Net Carbs
- 5 g Total Fats
- 2 g Total Protein
- 70 Calories

Fixings Needed:

- Blueberries (10)
- Yogurt (.5 cup)
- Vanilla extract (.5 tsp.)
- Coconut milk (1 cup)
- Stevia (as desired)

Preparation Method:

1. Add all of the ingredient components into the blender. Mix well.
2. When creamy smooth, pour into two chilled mugs and enjoy.

Chocolate Smoothie

Servings: 1 large
Total Prep & Cook Time: 5 minutes
Total Macro Nutrients per Serving:
- 4.4 g Net Carbs
- 46 g Total Fats
- 34.5 g Total Protein
- 570 Calories

Fixings Needed:

- Large eggs (2)
- Extra-virgin coconut oil (1 tbsp.)
- Almond or coconut butter (1-2 tbsp.)
- Coconut milk or heavy whipping cream (.25 cup)
- Chia seeds (1-2 tbsp.)
- Cinnamon (.5 tsp.)
- Stevia extract (3-5 drops)
- Plain or chocolate whey protein (.25 cup)
- Unsweetened cacao powder (1 tbsp.)
- Water (.25 cup)
- Vanilla extract (.5 tsp.)
- Ice (.5 cup)

Preparation Method:

1. Break the eggs along with the rest of fixings into the blender.
2. Pulse until frothy.
3. Add to a chilled glass and enjoy.

Chocolate Mint Smoothie

Servings: 1
Total Prep & Cook Time: 5-6 minutes
Total Macro Nutrients per Serving:
- 6.5 g Net Carbs
- 40 g Total Fats
- 5 g Total Protein
- 401 Calories

Fixings Needed:

- Medium avocado (5 of 1)
- Coconut milk (.25 cup)
- Unsweetened cashew/almond milk (1 cup)
- Swerve/erythritol (2 tbsp.)
- Cocoa powder (1 tbsp.)
- Fresh mint leaves (3-4)
- MCT oil (1 tbsp.)
- Ice cubes (2-3)
- Optional: Coconut milk or whipped cream

Preparation Method:

1. Mix all of the ingredients in your blender.
2. Add ice cubes, as many as you like. Add the topping if preferred.
3. Serve.

Chocolate & Raspberry Cheesecake Smoothie

Servings: 1
Total Prep & Cook Time: 5 minutes
Total Macro Nutrients per Serving:
- 7 g Net Carbs
- 54 g Total Fats
- 6.9 g Total Protein
- 512 Calories

Fixings Needed:

- Frozen or fresh raspberries (.33 cup)
- Coconut milk/heavy whipping cream (.25 cup)
- Full-fat cream cheese/creamed coconut milk (.25 cup)
- Unsweetened cacao powder (1 tbsp.)
- Extra-virgin coconut oil (1 tbsp.
- Water (.5 cup)
- Optional: Liquid stevia extract (3-5 drops)

Preparation Method:

1. Place all of the fixings for your smoothie in a blender.
2. Blend until frothy and smooth. Pour into a chilled glass and relax.

Cinnamon Smoothie

Servings: 1
Total Prep & Cook Time: 4 minutes
Total Macro Nutrients per Serving:
- 4.7 g Net Carbs
- 40.3 g Total Fats
- 23.6 g Total Protein
- 467 Calories

Fixings Needed:

- Cinnamon (.5 tsp.)
- Coconut milk (.5 cup)
- Water (.5 cup)
- Extra-virgin coconut oil or MCT oil (1 tbsp.)
- Ground chia seeds (1 tbsp.)
- Plain or vanilla whey protein (.25 cup)
- Stevia drops - optional (as desired)

Preparation Method:

1. Pour the milk, cinnamon, protein powder, and chia seeds in a blender.
2. Next, add coconut oil, ice, and water. Add a few drops of stevia if desired.
3. Pulse and serve.

Cinnamon Chocolate Smoothie

Servings: 1
Total Prep & Cook Time: 7-8 minutes
Total Macro Nutrients per Serving:
- 14 g Net Carbs
- 30 g Total Fats
- 3 g Total Protein
- 300 Calories

Fixings Needed:

- Coconut milk (.75 cup)
- Ripened avocado (.5 of 1)
- Cinnamon powder (1 tsp.)
- Unsweetened cacao powder (2 tsp.)
- Vanilla extract (.25 tsp.)
- Stevia (to taste)
- Optional: Coconut oil (1 tsp.) or MCT Oil (.5 tsp.)

Preparation Method:

1. Blend all of the above fixings and combine well.
2. Pour and serve when ready.

Cucumber & Spinach Smoothie

Servings: 1
Total Prep & Cook Time: 5 minutes
Total Macro Nutrients per Serving:
- 3.0 g Net Carbs
- 32 g Total Fats
- 10 g Total Protein
- 330 Calories

Fixings Needed:

- Cucumber (2.5 oz.)
- Spinach (2 handfuls)
- Coconut milk from a carton (1 cup)
- Xanthan gum (.25 tsp.)
- Liquid stevia (12 drops)
- MCT oil (1-2 tbsp.)
- Large cubes of ice (7)

Preparation Method:

1. Peel and cube the cucumber. Add it and the remainder of the ingredients into a blender. Puree the mixture for 1-2 minutes.
2. Serve when ready.

Easter Smoothie

Servings: 1
Total Prep & Cook Time: 8-10 minutes
Total Macro Nutrients per Serving:
- 10.8 g Net Carbs
- 23.3 g Total Fats
- 23.9 g Total Protein
- 364 Calories

Fixings Needed:

- Cantaloupe or honeydew (1 small wedge)
- Coconut milk or full-fat cream (.25 cup)
- Avocado (1/8 oz. or .25 of 1 average-sized)
- Psyllium/chia seeds (1 tbsp.)
- Kiwifruit or berries (.25 cup)
- Plain or vanilla whey protein (.25 cup)
- Liquid stevia extract (3-6 drops)
- Water (.5 cup)
- Ice cubes (2-3)

Preparation Method:

1. Cut the avocado in half and scoop out the insides. Add it to a blender.
2. Toss in the peeled melon, kiwi, and the rest of the fixings.
3. Blend well before serving.

Mexican Chocolate Smoothie

Servings: 1
Total Prep & Cook Time: 10 minutes
Total Macro Nutrients per Serving:
- 6.2 g Net Carbs
- 52.1 g Total Fats
- 6 g Total Protein
- 503 Calories

Fixings Needed:

- Extra-virgin coconut oil (2 tbsp.)
- Unsweetened cocoa powder (2 tbsp.)
- Coconut cream (.25 cup)
- Chia seeds (1 tbsp.)
- Cayenne powder (.25 tsp.)
- Cinnamon powder (.25 tsp.)
- Organic vanilla extract (.25 tsp.)
- Water (1 cup)
- Ice cubes (3-4)

Preparation Method:

1. Combine all of the fixings in your blender using the high-speed setting.
2. Mix until it's reached the desired consistency.

St. Patrick's Day Smoothie

Servings: 1
Total Prep & Cook Time: 10 minutes
Total Macro Nutrients per Serving:
- 9.4 g Net Carbs
- 37.1 g Total Fats
- 27.2 g Total Protein
- 493 Calories

Fixings Needed:

- Fresh baby spinach (.25 cup)
- Coconut milk or full-fat cream (.25 cup)
- Plain or vanilla whey protein/egg white protein powder (.25 cup)
- Medium avocado (3.5 oz. or .5 of 1)
- Vanilla bean (1) or (.5 - 1 tsp.) vanilla extract
- Unsalted pistachio nuts (2 tbsp.)
- Water (.5 cup)
- Liquid stevia extract (3-6 drops)
- Fresh mint/mint extract (to taste)
- Cubes of ice (if desired)

Preparation Method:

1. Rinse the spinach and mint. Drain in a colander.
2. Cut the avocado in half. Mix all of the fixings in a blender.
3. Serve when frothy.
4. Note: Add some ice during or after you combine the smoothie.

Strawberry Smoothie

Servings: 2
Total Prep & Cook Time: 5-6 minutes
Total Macro Nutrients per Serving:
- 5.1 g Net Carbs
- 6.6 g Total Fats
- 18.9 g Total Protein
- 156.8 Calories

Fixings Needed:

- Large strawberries (2)
- Unsweetened almond milk (16 oz.)
- Almonds (8)
- Whey protein powder (1.5 scoops)
- Cubes of ice (6)

Preparation Method:

1. Add all of the ingredients in your blender. Wait for the ice to break apart.
2. Serve in two 10-oz. chilled glasses. Yummy!

KETO SNACKS

Strawberry & Rhubarb Pie Smoothie

Servings: 1
Total Prep & Cook Time: 10 minutes
Total Macro Nutrients per Serving:
- 8.6 g Net Carbs
- 31.8 g Total Fats
- 14.2 g Total Protein
- 392 Calories

Fixings Needed:

- Almond butter (2 tbsp. or 1 oz. almonds)
- Medium rhubarb stalks (1.8 oz. - 1-2)
- Medium strawberries (2-4 or 1.4 oz.)
- Large organic/free-range egg (1)
- Coconut milk - full-fat cream (2 tbsp.)
- Unsweetened almond milk (.5 cup)
- Vanilla bean (1) or .5 tsp. pure vanilla bean extract
- Ginger root powder (.5 tsp.) or freshly grated ginger root (1 tsp.)
- Liquid stevia extract – vanilla or clear (3-6 drops)

Preparation Method:

1. Combine each of the ingredients into a blender.
2. Pulse and enjoy when smooth.

Tropical Smoothie

Servings: 2
Total Prep & Cook Time: 7-8 minutes
Total Macro Nutrients per Serving:
- 4.4 g Net Carbs
- 32.6 g Total Fats
- 4.4 g Total Protein
- 355.75 Calories

Fixings Needed:

- Unsweetened coconut milk (.75 cup)
- Sour cream (.25 cup)
- Large cubes of ice (7)
- Golden flaxseed meal (2 tbsp.)
- Liquid stevia (20 drops)
- MCT oil (1 tbsp.)
- Blueberry extract (.25 tsp.)
- Banana extract (.25 tsp.)
- Mango extract (.5 tsp.)

Preparation Method:

1. Combine all of the fixings in your blender (NutriBullet, for example, makes it easier.).
2. Wait a minute or two for the flax meal to soak some of the liquid.
3. Blend one to two minutes until well combined.
4. Serve and enjoy the taste of the tropics.

Frozen Treats

Cheesecake Popsicles

Servings: 12
Total Prep & Cook Time: 4 hours 15 minutes
Total Macro Nutrients per Serving:
- 3 .0g Net Carbs
- 12 g Total Fats
- 2 g Total Protein
- 122 Calories

Fixings Needed:

- Cream cheese (8 oz.)
- Cream (1 cup)
- Chopped strawberries (2 cups)
- Powdered swerve (.33 cup)
- Stevia extract (.25 tsp.)
- Lemon juice (1 tbsp.)
 Also Needed:
- Food Processor
- 12 wooden sticks
- Popsicle mold

Preparation Method:

1. Take the cream cheese out of the fridge to soften. Add to a food processor and pulse until smooth.
2. Pour in the cream, stevia, swerve, and juice. Mix well.
3. Add the berries (.5 of 1 cup at a time). Pour each one into a popsicle mold with a wooden stick.
4. Freeze at least 4 hours.

Chocolate Bon-bons

Servings: 6
Total Prep & Cook Time: 2 hours 15 minutes
Total Macro Nutrients per Serving:
- -0- g Net Carbs
- 10 g Total Fats
- 1 g Total Protein
- 100 Calories

Fixings Needed:

- Butter (5 tbsp.)
- Coconut oil (3 tbsp.
- Cocoa powder (2 tbsp.)
- Sugar-free raspberry syrup (2 tbsp.)

Preparation Method:

1. Mix the entire batch of ingredients in a pan.
2. Empty the bombs into six molds or muffin tins.
3. Place the tin into the freezer for a minimum of two hours.

CHAPTER 6

SWEET & TASTY KETO RECIPES FOR DESERTS

Pudding & Mousse Options

Almond Pumpkin Pudding

Servings: 10
Total Prep & Cook Time: 1 hour 20 minutes
Total Macro Nutrients per Serving:
- 4 g Net Carbs
- 16 g Total Fats
- 6 g Total Protein
- 154 Calories

Fixings Needed:

- Coconut oil (5 oz.)
- Ginger (.75 tsp.)
- Pumpkin pie spice (1 tbsp.)
- Powdered erythritol (3 tbsp.)

- Pumpkin puree (10 oz.)
- Coconut cream (5 oz.)
- Almonds (4 oz.)
- Also Needed: Silicone molds

Preparation Method:

1. Combine and stir all of the ingredients except for the almonds in a saucepan using the medium heat setting for about ten minutes.
2. Pour into the silicone molds and press an almond inside each one.
3. Freeze for a minimum of one hour. When they're ready, just remove from the molds.
4. Serve or freeze for later.

Cheesecake Pudding

Servings: 4
Total Prep & Cook Time: 10 minutes
Total Macro Nutrients per Serving:
- 5 g Net Carbs
- 36 g Total Fats
- 5 g Total Protein
- 356 Calories

Fixings Needed:

- Neufchatel cheese or Cream cheese (1 block)
- Heavy whipping cream (.5 cup)
- Lemon juice (1 tsp.)
- Sour cream (.5 cup)
- Liquid stevia (20 drops)
- Vanilla extract (1 tsp.

Preparation Method:

1. Microwave the cream cheese for 30 seconds or leave on the counter to soften for a few minutes before using.
2. Whip the sour cream and whipping cream together with a hand mixer until soft peaks form. Combine with the rest of the fixings and whip until fluffy.
3. Portion into four dishes to chill. Cover with plastic wrap in the fridge.

Chia Pudding

Servings: 4
Total Prep & Cook Time: 2-4 hours or overnight
Total Macro Nutrients per Serving:
- 12 g Net Carbs
- 24 g Total Fats
- 5 g Total Protein
- 273 Calories

Fixings Needed:

- Whole ripe avocado (1)
- Chia seeds (.25 cup)
- Medium dates (2)
- Almond or coconut milk (1 cup)
- Vanilla extract (.5 tsp.)

Preparation Method:

1. Pour the milk, vanilla, avocado, and dates into a blender.
2. Blend until well mixed. Empty over the chia seeds and cover overnight in the refrigerator when you go to bed. You can also let it chill for two to four hours before serving.

Lemon Custard

Servings: 4
Total Prep & Cook Time: 6 hours
Total Macro Nutrients per Serving:
- 3.0 g Net Carbs
- 30 g Total Fats
- 7 g Total Protein
- 319 Calories

Fixings Needed:

- Fresh lemon juice (.25 cup)
- Large egg yolks (5)
- Lemon zest (1 tbsp.)
- Liquid stevia (.5 tsp.)
- Vanilla extract (1 tsp.)
- Coconut cream/whipping cream (2 cups)
- Optional: Whipped coconut cream
- Also Needed: Slow Cooker & Ramekins or 4 small jars

Preparation Method:

1. Whisk the liquid stevia, egg yolks, lemon juice, lemon zest, and vanilla. Whip in the heavy cream. Divide into the jars.
2. Add a rack in the cooker and arrange the jars on top of it. Add water to fill half of the way up the sides of the ramekins.
3. Secure the lid and cook three hours on low.
4. Transfer the jars from the cooker and cool to room temperature. Chill in the fridge for approximately three hours.
5. Serve with the whipped cream if desired.

Cookies

Almond Nut Butter Cookies

Servings: 10
Total Prep & Cook Time: 25-30 minutes
Total Macro Nutrients per Serving:
- 7 g Net Carbs
- 22 g Total Fats
- 5 g Total Protein
- 235 Calories

Fixings Needed:

- Almond butter (8.8 oz.)
- Egg (1)
- Salted butter (.25 tsp.)
- Raw coconut butter (.25 cup)
- Powdered erythritol (.25 cup)

Preparation Method:

1. Warm up the oven to 320° Fahrenheit. Prepare a cookie sheet with a sheet of parchment paper.
2. Use a double boiler to melt the almond butter. Take it from the burner and stir in the salt, erythritol, and egg until well mixed.
3. Break into ten pieces and roll into balls.
4. Arrange on the prepared pan and flatten with a fork or your hand.
5. Bake for 12 minutes or until browned.

Amaretti Cookies

Servings: 16
Total Prep & Cook Time: 25 minutes
Total Macro Nutrients per Serving:
- 1 g Net Carbs
- 8 g Total Fats
- 2.5 g Total Protein
- 86 Calories

Fixings Needed:

- Coconut flour (2 tbsp.)
- Cinnamon (.25 tsp.)
- Baking powder (.5 tsp.)
- Erythritol (.5 cup)
- Salt (.5 tsp.)
- Almond flour (1 cup)
- Eggs (2)
- Almond extract (.5 tsp.)
- Vanilla extract (.5 tsp.)
- Coconut oil (4 tbsp.)
- Sugar-free jam (2 tbsp.)
- Shredded coconut (1 tbsp.)

Preparation Method:

1. Cover a baking tin with a sheet of parchment paper. Warm up the oven to reach 400° Fahrenheit.
2. Sift the flour and combine all of the dry fixings. After combined, work in the wet ones. Shape into 16 cookies. Make a dent in the center of each one. Bake for 15 to 17 minutes.
3. Let them cool a few minutes before adding a dab of jam to each one and a sprinkle of the coconut bits.

Chocolate Chip Cookies

Servings: 24
Total Prep & Cook Time: 55 minutes
Total Macro Nutrients per Serving:
- 2 g Net Carbs
- 8 g Total Fats
- 2 g Total Protein
- 90 Calories

Fixings Needed:

- Large egg (1)
- Swerve sweetener (.66 cup)
- Room temperature butter (5.5 tbsp.)
- Vanilla extract (.5 tsp.)
- Almond flour (1.25 cups)
- Sea salt - optional (.125 tsp.)
- Baking powder (1.5 tsp.)
- Coconut flour (1 tbsp.)
- Sugar-free chocolate chips (.5 cup)
- Optional: Molasses (.5 tsp.)
- Optional: Chopped pecans (.25 cup)

Preparation Method:

1. Use some parchment paper or silicone baking mats to line two baking sheets. Set the oven temperature to 325° Fahrenheit.
2. Use a mixer to blend the sweetener and butter. Stir in the molasses, egg, and vanilla extract until well combined.
3. In another container, combine the two flours, sea salt, and baking powder. Stir until blended. Fold in the pecans and chocolate chips.
4. Arrange the cookie dough by the tablespoonful into the prepared pans. They should be 1.5-inches apart.
5. Bake until the bottoms are browned or about 12-15 minutes. Let them cool until firm and set (minimum 25 minutes).

Chocolate Coconut Cookies

Servings: 20
Total Prep & Cook Time: 20-25 minutes
Total Macro Nutrients per Serving:
- 1 g Net Carbs
- 6.8 g Total Fats
- 2.2 g Total Protein
- 77 Calories

Fixings Needed:

- Almond flour (1 cup)
- Unsweetened shredded coconut (.33 cup)
- Erythritol (.33 cup)
- Baking powder (.5 tsp.)
- Cocoa powder (.25 cup)
- Coconut oil (.25 cup)
- Coconut flour (3 tbsp.)
- Salt (.25 tsp.)
- Vanilla extract (.25 tsp.)
- Un-chilled eggs (2)

Preparation Method:

1. Warm up the oven to 350° Fahrenheit. Cover a baking tin with a layer of parchment paper.
2. Mix the dry fixings using a hand mixer.
3. In another bowl, combine the wet ingredients and add to the dry until well blended.
4. Break apart pieces of the cookie dough and roll into 20 balls.
5. Arrange on the cookie sheet and bake for 15-20 minutes.

Cinnamon Cookies

Servings: 8
Total Prep & Cook Time: 35 minutes
Total Macro Nutrients per Serving:
- 6 g Net Carbs
- 25 g Total Fats
- 5 g Total Protein
- 260 Calories

Fixings Needed:

- Salted butter (.5 cup)
- Almond meal (2 cups)
- Stevia (.5 cup)
- Vanilla (1 tsp.)
- Cinnamon (1 tsp.)

Preparation Method:

1. Warm up the oven to reach 300° Fahrenheit.
2. Combine each of the fixings and shape into balls.
3. Prepare a cookie tin with a layer of parchment paper.
4. Arrange the cookies in the pan and press with a fork to flatten.
5. Bake for 20-25 minutes.

Delicious Homemade Graham Crackers

Servings: 10
Total Prep & Cook Time: 1 hour 5 minutes
Total Macro Nutrients per Serving:
- 3.53 g Net Carbs
- 13.4 g Total Fats
- 5.2 g Total Protein
- 156 Calories

Fixings Needed:

- Almond flour (2 cups)
- Swerve Brown or (.33 cup) regular Swerve & Molasses (2 tsp.) or Yacon syrup)
- Cinnamon (2 tsp.)
- Salt (1 pinch)
- Baking powder (1 tsp.)
- Large egg (1)
- Melted butter (2 tbsp.)
- Vanilla extract (1 tsp.)

Preparation Method:

1. Warm up the oven to reach 300° Fahrenheit.
2. Whisk the cinnamon, almond flour, baking powder, sweetener, and salt.
3. Whip and mix in the egg, molasses, melted butter, and vanilla extract. Turn the dough out onto a large piece of parchment paper or silicone liner and pat into a rough rectangle.
4. Top the dough with another piece of parchment. Roll out dough as evenly as possible to approximately ⅛-¼-inch thickness.
5. Remove the top paper and score (not cut) into squares of about 2 by 2 inches. Arrange on a baking sheet.
6. Bake for 20 to 30 minutes, until just beginning to brown.
7. Remove the crackers and cool 30 minutes. Break up along the scored marks. Return to the warm oven with the oven off or no higher than 200° Fahrenheit.
8. Cool another 30 minutes, and then cool until crispy.

Ginger Snap Cookies

Servings: 1
Total Prep & Cook Time: 25 minutes
Total Macro Nutrients per Serving:
- 2.2 g Net Carbs
- 6.7 g Total Fats
- 2.25 g Total Protein
- 74 Calories

Fixings Needed:

- Ground cloves (.25 tsp.)
- Nutmeg (.25 tsp.)
- Salt (.25 tsp.)
- Almond flour (2 cups)
- Ground cinnamon (.5 tsp.)
- Unsalted butter (.25 cup)
- Vanilla extract (1 tsp.)
- Large egg (1)

Preparation Method:

1. Warm up the oven temperature to 350° Fahrenheit.
2. Whisk the dry fixings in a mixing bowl. Blend in the rest of the ingredients into the dry mixture using a hand blender. The dough will be stiff.
3. Measure out the dough for each cookie and flatten with a fork or your fingers.
4. Bake for about 9 to 11 minutes or until browned.

Macaroons

Servings: 1
Total Prep & Cook Time: 20 minutes
Total Macro Nutrients per Serving:
- 4 g Net Carbs
- 10 g Total Fats
- 2 g Total Protein
- 90 Calories

Ingredients:

- Egg whites (4)
- Water (4.5 tsp.)
- Vanilla (1 tsp.)
- Artificial sweetener of choice (1 cup)
- Unsweetened coconut (.5 cup)

Preparation Method:

1. Program the oven to 325° Fahrenheit.
2. Whisk the eggs with the liquid ingredients. Stir in the coconut and mix well. Use an immersion blender for uniform consistency.
3. Add the batter into the greased pan.
4. Bake for 15 minutes.

Orange Walnut Cookies

Servings: 10
Total Prep & Cook Time: 60 minutes
Total Macro Nutrients per Serving:
- 4 g Net Carbs
- 17 g Total Fats
- 7 g Total Protein
- 137 Calories

Fixings Needed:

- Walnut halves (8 oz.)
- Orange - zested (3 tbsp.)
- Eggs (1)
- Stevia drops (20)
- Cinnamon to garnish (1 pinch)
- Shredded coconut - to garnish (to taste)

Preparation Method:

1. Set the oven temperature to about 320° Fahrenheit.
2. Toast the walnuts for about 10 minutes until browned. Add them to a food processor. Toss in the rest of the fixings and continue blending until it's smooth.
3. Shape into ten balls and slightly flatten. Drizzle with a portion of the shredded coconut.
4. Bake for 40 minutes. Cool on the rack a few minutes and add to a platter to finish cooling.
5. Store in an airtight container and enjoy any time.

P B & J Cookies

Servings: 6
Total Prep & Cook Time: 20 minutes
Total Macro Nutrients per Serving:
- 5 g Net Carbs
- 18 g Total Fats
- 9 g Total Protein
- 209 Calories

Fixings Needed:

- Egg (1)
- Stevia sugar substitute (.5 cup)
- Creamy keto-friendly peanut butter (.66 cup)
- Sugar-free strawberry preserves (.33 cup)
- Almond flour (.33 cup)
- Sea salt (.25 tsp.)
- Baking powder (.25 tsp.)
- Pure vanilla extract (.25 tsp.)

Preparation Method:

1. Warm up the oven to 350° Fahrenheit. Spray a cookie sheet with a spritz of cooking oil or prepare with a layer of parchment paper.
2. Whisk the egg and combine with the stevia and peanut butter. When it's creamy, add the salt, baking powder, flour, and vanilla.
3. Mix well and shape into small balls. Make an indention in each one and add one teaspoon of preserves.
4. Bake until browned or for about 10 to 12 minutes.
5. Cool on a wire rack and serve.

Pistachio Cookies

Servings: 16
Total Prep & Cook Time: 45 minutes
Total Macro Nutrients per Serving:
- 2 g Net Carbs
- 12 g Total Fats
- 4 g Total Protein
- 135 Calories

Fixings Needed:

- Melted butter (6 tbsp.)
- Chopped pistachios (.5 cup)
- Erythritol (.5 cup)
- Almond flour (2 cups)

Preparation Method:

1. Combine all of the ingredients together in a mixing container.
2. Shape the dough into a long roll and cover with a sheet of plastic wrap.
3. Place in the fridge for about ½ hour. Unwrap and slice into 16 portions.
4. Bake for 12 to 15 minutes.

Walnut Cookies

Servings: 16
Total Prep & Cook Time: 23 minutes
Total Macro Nutrients per Serving:
- 1.1 g Net Carbs
- 6.7 g Total Fats
- 3 g Total Protein
- 72 Calories

Fixings Needed:

- Egg (1)
- Ground cinnamon (1 tsp.)
- Erythritol (2 tbsp.)
- Ground walnuts (1.5 cups)

Preparation Method:

1. Warm up the oven to reach 356° Fahrenheit.
2. Combine the cinnamon and erythritol with the egg.
3. Fold in the walnuts.
4. Shape into balls and place on a parchment paper-lined baking tin.
5. Bake for 10 to 13 minutes.

Muffins

Apple Cinnamon Muffins

Servings: 12
Total Prep & Cook Time: 25-30 minutes
Total Macro Nutrients per Serving:
- 3.0 g Net Carbs
- 22 g Total Fats
- 7 g Total Protein
- 241 Calories

Fixings Needed:

- Nutmeg (1 tsp.)
- Cinnamon (3 tbsp.)
- Almond flour (3 cups)
- Cloves (.25 tsp.)
- Baking powder (1 tsp.)
- Lemon juice (1 tsp.)
- Stevia (to your liking)
- Melted ghee (.5 cup)
- Large whisked eggs (3)
- Applesauce (4 tbsp.)
- Also Needed: 12-count muffin tins & paper or silicone cups

Preparation Method

1. Warm up the oven to 350° Fahrenheit.
2. Combine the rest of the ingredients in a mixing bowl.
3. Pour the batter into the prepared muffin tins.
4. Bake for 17 to 20 minutes or until the center springs back when touched lightly.

Brownie Muffins

Servings: 6
Total Prep & Cook Time: 20 minutes
Total Macro Nutrients per Serving:
- 4.4 g Net Carbs
- 13 g Total Fats
- 7 g Total Protein
- 183 Calories

Fixings Needed:

- Salt (.5 tsp.)
- Flaxseed meal (1 cup)
- Cocoa powder (.25 cup)
- Cinnamon (1 tbsp.)
- Baking powder (.5 tbsp.)
- Coconut oil (2 tbsp.)
- Large egg (1)
- Sugar-free caramel syrup (.25 cup)
- Vanilla extract (1 tsp.)
- Pumpkin puree (.5 cup)
- Slivered almonds (.5 cup)
- Apple cider vinegar (1 tsp.)

Preparation Method:

1. Set the oven temperature to 350° Fahrenheit.
2. Use a deep mixing container to mix all of the fixings and stir well.
3. Place 6 paper liners in the muffin tin and add 1/4 cup of batter to each one.
4. Sprinkle several almonds on the tops, pressing gently. Bake for approximately 15 minutes or until the top is set.

One-Minute Muffin

Servings: 1
Total Prep & Cook Time: 3 minutes
Total Macro Nutrients per Serving:
- 6.3 g Net Carbs
- 15 g Total Fats
- 8.9 g Total Protein
- 377 Calories

Fixings Needed:

- Almond flour (2 tbsp.)
- Flaxseed meal (2 tbsp.)
- Baking powder (.5 tsp.)
- Salt (1 pinch)
- Oil (1 tsp.)
- Egg (1)

Preparation Method:

1. Combine each of the dry fixings. Work in the oil and egg.
2. Microwave for one minute or bake at 350° Fahrenheit for 15 minutes. Serve.

Pumpkin Maple Flaxseed Muffins

Servings: 10
Total Prep & Cook Time: 30 minutes
Total Macro Nutrients per Serving:
- 2 g Net Carbs
- 8.5 g Total Fats
- 5 g Total Protein
- 120 Calories

Fixings Needed:

- Ground flaxseeds (1.25 cups)
- Baking powder (.5 tbsp.)
- Erythritol (.33 cup)
- Salt (.5 tsp.)
- Cinnamon (1 tbsp.)
- Pumpkin pie spice (1 tbsp.)
- Coconut oil (2 tbsp.)
- Pure pumpkin puree (1 cup)
- Egg (1)
- Maple syrup (.5 tsp.)
- Apple cider vinegar (.5 tsp.)
- Vanilla extract (.5 tsp.)
- Garnish: Pumpkin seeds
  Also Needed:
- Blender such as NutriBullet
- Muffin tin – 10-count sections with silicone liners

Preparation Method:

1. Preheat the oven to 350° Fahrenheit.
2. Prepare the muffin tin with cupcake liners.
3. Add the seeds to the blender about one second – no longer or it could become damp.
4. Combine the dry fixings and whisk until well mixed.
5. Add the vanilla extract, puree, and pumpkin spice along with the maple syrup if using.

6. Blend in the oil, egg, and apple cider vinegar.
7. Combine nuts or any other fold-ins of your choice, but also add the carbs.
8. Scoop the mixture out by the tablespoon into the prepared tins.
9. Garnish with some of the pumpkin seeds. Leave a little space in the top since they'll rise. Bake for approximately 20 minutes or until they are slightly browned.
10. Let them cool for a few minutes and add some ghee or butter or some more syrup.

Pies

Blueberry Cream Pie

Servings: 16
Total Prep & Cook Time: 3 hours 30 minutes
Total Macro Nutrients per Serving:
- 3.0 g Net Carbs
- 30 g Total Fats
- 5.4 g Total Protein
- 305 Calories

Fixings Needed:

- Unsweetened shredded coconut (1 cup)
- Unsalted sunflower seeds (1 cup)
- Salt (.25 tsp.)
- Softened butter (.25 cup)

Filling Fixings Needed:

- Fresh or frozen blueberries (1 cup)
- Gelatin (2.5 tsp or 1 envelope)
- Lemon juice (2 tbsp.)
- Water (2 tbsp.)
- Swerve sweetener (.75 tsp.)
- Softened cream cheese (16 oz.)
- Liquid stevia (.5 tsp.)
- Heavy cream – divided (2 cups)

Topping Ingredients:

- Heavy cream (1 cup)
- Blueberry mixture – reserved from the filling (.25 cup)

- Vanilla liquid stevia (.5 tsp.)
- Also Needed: 8 x 8 baking dish

Preparation Method:

1. Mix all of the crust fixings in a food processor and pulse until combined. Coat the baking dish with a spritz non-stick cooking oil spray. Add the crust.
2. Process the lemon juice and berries in the food processor until chopped.
3. Pour the water into a pan. Once it starts boiling, add the gelatin, stir, and set aside to cool.
4. In a stand mixer, add the cream cheese, 3/4 cup of the berries, lemon stevia, and swerve – mixing until smooth.
5. Stir in 1 cup of the heavy cream and blend two to three minutes. Drizzle with the gelatin and mix. Pour into the crust.
6. Add the other cup of heavy cream along with the rest of the berries and blend on the high setting in the mixture to form the topping.
7. Decorate the pie with the filling and chill in the fridge for two or three hours. When ready to eat, decorate with a few berries.

Creamy Lime Pie

Servings: 9
Total Prep & Cook Time: 25 minutes (+) chill time
Total Macro Nutrients per Serving:
- 4.2 g Net Carbs
- 39 g Total Fats
- 7 g Total Protein
- 386 Calories

Fixings Needed:

- Melted butter (.25 cup)
- Almond flour (1.5 cups)
- Salt (.5 tsp.)
- Erythritol – divided (.5 cup)
- Heavy cream (1 cup)
- Egg yolks (4)
- Freshly squeezed key lime juice (.33 cup)
- Lime zest (1 tbsp.)
- Cubed cold butter (.25 cup)
- Vanilla extract (1 tsp.)
- Sour cream (1 cup)
- Cream cheese (.5 cup)
- Xanthan gum (.25 tsp.)

Preparation Method:

1. Warm up the oven to 350° Fahrenheit.
2. Melt the butter in a pan.
3. Combine the salt, half or 1/4 cup of the erythritol, and the almond flour. Slowly add the butter. Blend and press into a pie platter.
4. Bake for 15 minutes.
5. Remove when it's lightly browned. Let it cool.

6. In another saucepan, combine the egg yolks, heavy cream, rest of the erythritol, lime zest, and juice. Simmer over medium heat for 7 to 10 minutes or until it starts to thicken.
7. Take the pan from the burner. Stir in the xanthan gum, vanilla extract, cold butter, cream cheese, and sour cream. Whisk until smooth. Scoop into the cooled pie shell.
8. Cover and place in the fridge for four hours or leave it overnight.

Mini Coconut Pies

Servings: 12
Total Prep & Cook Time: 50 minutes
Total Macro Nutrients per Serving:
- 3.0 g Net Carbs
- 13 g Total Fats
- 3 g Total Protein
- 174 Calories

Fixings Needed:

- Coconut oil (1 tbsp.)
- Coconut flour (1 cup)
- Large eggs (2)
- Melted ghee (.5 cup)
- Sugar-free vanilla bean sweetener (3 tbsp.)
- Unsweetened coconut cream (1 cup)
- Unsweetened shredded coconut (.25 cup)
- Also Needed: 12-count mini muffin tin

Preparation Method:

1. Warm up the oven to 350° Fahrenheit.
2. Lightly grease the cups of the tin with coconut oil.
3. In a mixing bowl, whisk together the eggs, ghee, coconut flour, and 1 tablespoon of the vanilla bean sweetener.
4. Portion the flour mixture between the mini-muffin cups and pat into the bottom of each cup. Bake for 10 minutes.
5. Cool completely and remove the little coconut pie shells from the tin.
6. In a small mixing bowl, mix the shredded coconut, coconut cream, and the remaining 2 tablespoons of sweetener.
7. Top each pie shell with about 1 tbsp of the cream mixture. Chill the pies for at least 30 minutes before serving.
8. Top with a portion of toasted coconut to your liking before serving.

Pumpkin Cheesecake Pie

Servings: 8
Total Prep & Cook Time: 40-45 minutes (+) chill time
Total Macro Nutrients per Serving:
- 6 g Net Carbs
- 44 g Total Fats
- 10 g Total Protein
- 460 Calories

Fixings Needed:

- Almond flour (1.75 cups)
- Cinnamon (.5 tsp.)
- Swerve (3 tbsp.)
- Melted butter (1 stick)

Fixings Needed For The Filling:

- Pumpkin puree (.66 cup)
- Swerve (.66 cup)
- Vanilla extract (.5 tsp.)
- Cinnamon (.5 tsp.)
- Nutmeg (.25 tsp.)
- Allspice (.125 tsp.)
- Room-temperature large eggs (2)
- Room-temperature - cream cheese (16 oz.)
- Also Needed: (1) 9-inch pie plate

Preparation Method:

1. Prepare the crust. Combine the cinnamon, sweetener, and almond flour in the baking dish. Melt and stir in the butter. Press the fixings together.
2. Prepare the filling. Mix the sweetener, vanilla, and cream cheese with an electric mixer. When smooth blend in the

pumpkin, nutmeg, eggs, cinnamon, and allspice.
3. Scrape the filling into the prepared crust. Bake for 35-40 minutes. Remove when the filling is firm.
4. Set aside to cool down on a wire rack. Chill overnight or for at least a few hours before serving in equal portions.

Other Delicious Sweet Treats

Almond Chia Bars

Servings: 14
Total Prep & Cook Time: 1 hour 30 minutes
Total Macro Nutrients per Serving:
- 1.5 g Net Carbs
- 11 g Total Fats
- 2.5 g Total Protein
- 121 Calories

Fixings Needed:

- Toasted almonds (.5 cup)
- Coconut oil (divided – 1 tbsp. (+) 1 tsp.)
- Erythritol (4 tbsp. - divided)
- Butter (2 tbsp.)
- Liquid stevia (.25 tsp.)
- Vanilla extract (1.5 tsp.)
- Heavy cream (.25 tsp.)
- Unsweetened & shredded coconut flakes (.5 cup)
- Chia seeds (.25 cup)
- Coconut cream (.5 cup)
- Coconut flour (2 tbsp.)
- Also Needed: Food Processor

Preparation Method:

1. Add the toasted almonds into the food processor and pulse until crumbly.
2. Toss in 1 tablespoon of the coconut oil and 2 tablespoons of the erythritol. Continue processing until you have almond butter.

KETO SNACKS

3. Warm up a pan and add the butter, heavy cream, erythritol, stevia, and vanilla. Stir until bubbly and fold in the almond butter. Stir to blend.
4. In a blender, grind the chia seeds to make a powdery mix.
5. In another pan, toast the coconut flakes and mix with the chia seeds.
6. Melt the coconut cream in a separate skillet.
7. Combine all of the fixings and add the melted coconut cream, flour, and coconut oil. Store in the refrigerator for one hour.
8. Slice into squares and store in the refrigerator.

Apple Cider Donut Bites

Servings: 12
Total Prep & Cook Time: 30 minutes
Total Macro Nutrients per Serving - 2 bites each:
- 2.58 g Net Carbs
- 17.71 g Total Fats
- 6.52 g Total Protein
- 164 Calories

Fixings Needed For The Donut Bites:

- Almond flour (2 cups)
- Swerve Sweetener (.5 cup)
- Unflavoured whey protein powder (.25 cup)
- Baking powder (2 tsp.)
- Cinnamon (.5 tsp.)
- Salt (.5 tsp.)
- Large eggs (2)
- Water (.33 cup)
- Butter melted (.25 cup)
- Apple cider vinegar (1.5 tbsp.)
- Apple extract (1.5 tsp.)

Fixings Needed For The Coating:

- Swerve Sweetener (.25 cup)
- Cinnamon (1-2 tsp.)
- Butter - melted (.25 cup)
- Also Needed: 24- count mini muffin pan

Preparation Method:

1. Preheat the oven to 325° Fahrenheit. Lightly grease the pan.
2. Whisk together the almond flour, protein powder, sweetener, baking powder, cinnamon, and salt.
3. Whisk in the eggs and water with the butter, apple cider vinegar, and apple extract.
4. Divide the mixture among the wells of the pan.
5. Bake for 15 to 20 minutes or until the muffins are firm to the touch. Remove and let cool for 10 minutes, then transfer to a wire rack to cool completely.
6. In a small container, whisk together the sweetener and cinnamon.
7. Dip each donut bite into the melted butter, coating completely.
8. Roll each donut bite into the cinnamon/sweetener mixture.

Baked Apples

Servings: 4
Total Prep & Cook Time: 1 hour 10 minutes
Total Macro Nutrients per Serving:
- 16 g Net Carbs
- 19.9 g Total Fats
- 6.8 g Total Protein
- 175 Calories

Fixings Needed:

- Keto-friendly sweetener (4 tsp. or to taste)
- Cinnamon (.75 tsp.)
- Chopped pecans (.25 cup)
- Granny Smith apples (4 large)

Preparation Method:

1. Set the oven temperature at 375° Fahrenheit.
2. Mix the sweetener with the cinnamon and pecans.
3. Core the apple and add the prepared stuffing.
4. Add enough water into the baking dish to cover the bottom of the apple.
5. Bake for about 45 minutes to 1 hour.

Baked Brie & Almonds

Servings: 8
Total Prep & Cook Time: 25 minutes
Total Macro Nutrients per Serving:
- 8 g Total Carbs
- 12 g Total Fats
- 8.4 g Total Protein
- 187 Calories

Fixings Needed:

- Toasted almonds (.5 cup)
- Brie cheese (14 oz. round)
- Fresh figs (6)
- Liquid stevia (1 tbsp.)
- Water (2 tbsp.)

Preparation Method:

1. Warm up the oven to 325° Fahrenheit.
2. Heat up a saucepan of water with the stevia and figs.
3. Simmer until softened and stir in the almonds.
4. Arrange the cheese in the baking dish. Pour the almond mixture over its top.
5. Bake for 15 minutes.

Blueberry Tart

Servings: 9
Total Prep & Cook Time: 30 minutes
Total Macro Nutrients per Serving:
- 5.9 g Net Carbs
- 8.3 g Total Fats
- 1.1 g Total Protein
- 103 Calories

Fixings Needed:

- Blueberries (3 cups)
- Almond flour (.66 cup)
- Coconut flour (.33 cup)
- Melted butter (6 tbsp.)
- Egg (1)
- Powdered sweetener of choice (.25 cup)
- Lemon juice (1 tbsp.)

Preparation Method:

1. Warm up the oven to reach 350° Fahrenheit.
2. Lightly grease a baking pan and add the berries with a sprinkle of the lemon juice.
3. Whisk the coconut and almond flour with the sweetener and the egg.
4. Pour the mixture over the prepared berries with a drizzle of the melted butter.
5. Bake for 25 minutes.

Cheesecake Cupcakes

Servings: 12
Total Prep & Cook Time: 20-25 minutes (+) 8 hours wait time
Total Macro Nutrients per Serving:
- 2.1 g Net Carbs
- 20 g Total Fats
- 4.9 g Total Protein
- 204 Calories

Fixings Needed:

- Melted butter (.25 cup)
- Almond meal (.5 cup)
- Eggs (2)
- Softened cream cheese (16 oz. pkg.)
- Stevia or your favorite sweetener (.75 cup)
- Vanilla extract (1 tsp.)

Preparation Method:

1. Warm up the oven until it reaches 350° Fahrenheit. Prepare a muffin tin with 12 paper liners.
2. Combine the butter and almond meal. Spoon into the cups to make a flat crust.
3. Whisk the vanilla, sweetener of choice, eggs, and cream cheese with an electric mixer until creamy. Scoop it in on top of the crust. Bake for 15-17 minutes.
4. Once they're done the cooking cycle, just remove and cool at room temperature. Store overnight or at least 8 hours.

Cheesecake Mocha Bars

Servings: 16
Total Prep & Cook Time: 50-55 minutes
Total Macro Nutrients per Serving:
- 3.24 g Net Carbs
- 21.2 g Total Fats
- 6.1 g Total Protein
- 232 Calories

Fixings Needed for The Brownie Layer:

- Vanilla extract (2 tsp.)
- Unsalted butter (6 tbsp.)
- Large eggs (3)
- Salt (.5 tsp.)
- Instant coffee (.5 tbsp.)
- Baking powder (1 tsp.)
- Almond flour (1.5 cups)
- Hershey's Baking Cocoa or your favorite (.5 cup)
- Erythritol (1 cup)

Fixings Needed For The Cream Cheese Layer:

- Softened cream cheese (1 lb.)
- Erythritol (.5 cup)
- Large egg (1)
- Vanilla extract (1 tsp.)
- Also Needed: 8x8-inch baking pan

Preparation Method:

1. Set the oven temperature to 350° Fahrenheit. Lightly grease or spray the pan.
2. Combine the wet fixings starting with the vanilla and butter. Mix in the eggs.

3. In another container, combine the dry ingredients and whisk in with the wet fixings. Set aside 1/4 cup of the batter for later. Pour the mixture into the pan.
4. Mix the room temperature cream cheese with the rest of the fixings for the second layer. Spread it on the sheet of brownies.
5. Use the reserved batter as the last layer (it will be thin).
6. Bake for 30-35 minutes. When cooled, slice the cheesecake bars, and serve or store for later.

Coconut Bars

Servings: 20
Total Prep & Cook Time: 15 minutes
Total Macro Nutrients per Serving:
- 2 g Net Carbs
- 11 g Total Fats
- 2 g Total Protein
- 108 Calories

Fixings Needed:

- Unsweetened shredded coconut (3 cups)
- Coconut oil (1 cup)
- Liquid sweetener of choice (.25 cup)

Preparation Method:

1. Line a pan with a layer of parchment paper.
2. Combine the ingredients to make a thick batter.
3. Pour into the pan and freeze until firm.
4. Cut into squares and store until you want a delicious snack.

Coconut & Chocolate Bites

Servings: 6
Total Prep & Cook Time: 2 hours 30 minutes
Total Macro Nutrients per Serving:
- 9 g Net Carbs
- 27 g Total Fats
- 9 g Total Protein
- 326 Calories

Fixings Needed:

- Unsweetened 80% or higher dark chocolate (4 oz.)
- Heavy cream (.33 cup)
- Coconut flour (1 cup)
- Chocolate protein powder (1 tbsp.)
- Shredded unsweetened coconut (.25 cup)
- Coconut oil (4 tbsp.)

Preparation Method:

1. Dice the dark chocolate into bits.
2. Warm up the heavy cream in a saucepan (medium-low). Stir in the chocolate bits and oil. Continue stirring until combined and remove from the burner.
3. Stir in the protein powder and coconut flour. Store in the refrigerator for a minimum of two hours.
4. Take the dough out of the fridge when it's cool. Shape into balls and roll through the shredded coconut until coated.
5. Store in the fridge in a closed container.

Coconut Cream Brownies

Servings: 6
Total Prep & Cook Time: 30 minutes
Total Macro Nutrients per Serving:
- 2 g Net Carbs
- 17 g Total Fats
- 3 g Total Protein
- 175 Calories

Fixings Needed:

- Coconut cream (.33 cup)
- Melted coconut butter (.75 cup)
- Raw - unsweetened cocoa powder (.33 cup)
- Coconut flour (.33 cup)
- Melted butter/coconut oil (2 tbsp.)
- Sugar substitute - stevia (.5 cup)
- Pure vanilla extract (1 tsp.)
- Sea salt (1 pinch)
- Egg (1)
- Baking soda (.25 tsp.)
- Also Needed: 9x3-inch loaf pan

Preparation Method:

1. Heat up the oven until it reaches 350° Fahrenheit.
2. Combine the stevia, salt, flour, cocoa powder, and baking powder.
3. Whisk the coconut cream and butter in another container. When combined, mix in the vanilla and the whisked egg.
4. Combine all of the fixings and add to the baking pan.
5. Bake for 20 minutes.
6. Once it's done, just cool and slice into six equal squares.

Cream Cheese Truffles

Servings: 24
Total Prep & Cook Time: 2 hours
Total Macro Nutrients per Serving:
- 2.2 g Net Carbs
- 7 g Total Fats
- 1.23 g Total Protein
- 72.7 Calories

Fixings Needed:

- Softened cream cheese (16 oz.)
- Unsweetened cocoa powder (.5 cup - divided)
- Swerve confectioners (4 tbsp.)
- Liquid Stevia (.25 tsp.)
- Rum extract (.5 tsp.)
- Instant coffee (1 tbsp.)
- Water (2 tbsp.)
- Heavy whipping cream (1 tbsp.)
- Paper candy cups for serving (24)

Preparation Method:

1. Combine about one-quarter of a cup of the cocoa powder with the rest of the ingredients.
2. Whisk them with an electric mixer and chill in the fridge for about 30 minutes before rolling them out.
3. Sprinkle the rest of the cocoa powder on the counter and roll out the balls (by the tablespoons) with your hands. Roll them in the powder and place them in the candy cups.
4. Chill for an additional hour before serving.

Peanut Butter & Coconut Balls

Servings: 15
Total Prep & Cook Time: 65 minutes (+) overnight chill time
Total Macro Nutrients per Serving:
- 0.92 g Net Carbs
- 3.2 g Total Fats
- 0.98 g Total Protein
- 35 Calories

Fixings Needed:

- Powdered erythritol (2.5 tsp.)
- Unsweetened cocoa powder (3 tsp.)
- Creamy peanut butter – keto-friendly (3 tbsp.)
- Almond flour (2 tsp.)
- Unsweetened coconut flakes (.5 cup)

Preparation Method:

1. Combine the peanut butter, cocoa, erythritol, and flour. Place in the freezer for one hour.
2. Spoon out a small spoon size of the peanut butter mix. Roll into the flakes until it is covered.
3. Refrigerate overnight for the best results and enjoy.

Pumpkin Bars with Cream Cheese Frosting

Servings: 16
Total Prep & Cook Time: 55-60 minutes
Total Macro Nutrients per Serving:
- 2 g Net Carbs
- 13 g Total Fats
- 3 g Total Protein
- 139 Calories

Fixings Needed:

- Large eggs (2)
- Coconut oil (.25 cup)
- Cream cheese (2 oz.)
- Pumpkin puree (1 cup)
- Almond flour (1 cup)
- Vanilla extract (1 tsp.)
- Gluten-free baking powder (2 tsp.)
- Erythritol sweetener blend (.66 cups
- Pumpkin pie spice (1 tsp.)
- Sea salt (.5 tsp.)

Ingredients for the Frosting:

- Powdered erythritol (.5 cup)
- Optional: Heavy cream (1 tbsp.)
- Softened cream cheese (6 oz.)
- Vanilla extract (1 tsp.)
- Also Needed: 9 x 9 baking pan

Preparation Method:

1. Warm up the oven until it reaches 350° Fahrenheit. Cover the baking pan with parchment paper.
2. In a double boiler or microwave, melt the coconut oil and cream cheese.

3. Combine the vanilla, eggs, cream cheese mixture, and puree using a hand mixer until smooth using the medium-speed setting.
4. Whisk the dry fixings (salt, pie spice, baking powder, sweetener, and flour).
5. Mix all the ingredients with the mixer until just combined and pour into the pan.
6. Bake for 20 to 30 minutes. Cool completely.
7. Prepare the frosting with each of the ingredients when the bars are cooled. If it's too thick, just add a little cream or milk.
8. Slice into 16 equal portions. Enjoy any time.

Pumpkin Blondies

Servings: 12
Total Prep & Cook Time: 35-40 minutes
Total Macro Nutrients per Serving:
- 1.5 g Net Carbs
- 11 g Total Fats
- 2 g Total Protein
- 110 Calories

Fixings Needed:

- Coconut oil (as needed for the pan)
- Egg (1 large)
- Softened butter (.5 cup)
- Pumpkin puree (.5 cup)
- Erythritol (.5 cup)
- Almond flour (.25 cup)
- Coconut flour (2 tbsp.)
- Cinnamon (1 tsp.)
- Pumpkin pie spice (.125 tsp.)
- Liquid stevia (15 drops)
- Maple extract (1 tsp.)
- Chopped pecans (1 oz.)

Preparation Method:

1. Heat up the oven temperature to 350° Fahrenheit. Grease a baking pan with a spritz of coconut oil.
2. Mix the egg, butter, puree, and erythritol with an electric mixer.
3. Combine each of the flours with the pie spice, stevia, cinnamon, and maple extract.
4. Blend it all together and add to the prepared pan. Sprinkle the top with pecans.
5. Bake for 20-25 minutes until the edges are lightly browned.

Strawberry & Cream Cakes

Servings: 5
Total Prep & Cook Time: 45 minutes
Total Macro Nutrients per Serving:
- 3.7 g Net Carbs
- 30 g Total Fats
- 6 g Total Protein
- 275 Calories

Fixings Needed:

- Eggs (3)
- Cream cheese (3 oz./6 tbsp.)
- Vanilla extract (.5 tsp.)
- Baking powder (.25 tsp.)
- Erythritol (2 tbsp.)

Ingredients for The Filling:

- Strawberries (10)
- Heavy cream (1 cup)

Preparation Method:

1. Cover a baking sheet with parchment paper.
2. Break the eggs and which just the egg *whites*. Whisk to form stiff peaks.
3. In another dish; combine the cream cheese, egg *yolks*, vanilla extract, baking powder, and erythritol.
4. Slowly add the egg mixtures together. Shape into cake forms and place on the lined baking tin.
5. Whip the heavy cream until thickened.
6. Bake for 25-30 minutes.
7. Let them cool and add the berries and cream.

Strawberry Gummies

Servings: 4
Total Prep & Cook Time: 2 hours
Total Macro Nutrients per Serving:
- 3.0 g Net Carbs
- 4 g Total Fats
- 4 g Total Protein
- 39 Calories

Fixings Needed:

- Fresh strawberries (7 oz.)
- Unsweetened almond milk or other non-dairy milk (1 cup)
- Liquid sweetener - stevia glycerite (.5 tsp.)
- Vanilla extract (.5 tsp.)
- Lemon zest (.5 tsp.)
- Salt (1 pinch)
- Unflavored powdered gelatin (2 tbsp.)
- Also Needed: Silicone molds

Preparation Method:

1. In a blender, combine the berries and milk until liquified. Pour through a fine-mesh sieve to strain out the seeds.
2. Warm the strawberry milk using the medium heat temperature setting in a saucepan. Whisk in the vanilla, lemon zest, stevia, and salt. Taste test and sweeten as desired.
3. Once steaming, pour it back into the blender.
4. Add the gelatin and blend using the low setting for 15 seconds. Pour the mixture into the silicone mold and put in the refrigerator to set for 1.5 hours.
5. When firm, remove them from the fridge and unmold them. Serve chilled.

Strawberry Rhubarb Crumble

Servings: 8
Total Prep & Cook Time: 45-55 minutes
Total Macro Nutrients per Serving:
- 3.5 g Net Carbs
- 20.6 g Total Fats
- 4.2 g Total Protein
- 230 Calories

Fixings Needed For The Filling:

- Strawberries (1 cup)
- Rhubarb (1 cup)
- Lemon juice (1 tbsp.)
- Steviva Blend or your favorite stevia/erythritol baking blend (1-2 tsp)
- Xanthan gum (.5 tsp.)

Fixings Needed For The Crumble:

- Walnuts (1 cup)
- Coconut flour (.5 cup)
- Flaxseed meal (.25 cup)
- Steviva Blend (or your favorite stevia/erythritol baking blend (.25 cup (+) 1 tsp.)
- Melted unsalted butter (6 tbsp.)
- Sea salt (.25 tsp.)
- Also Needed: 9-inch glass pie plate

Preparation Method:

1. Finely dice the rhubarb, walnuts, and strawberries.
2. Warm up the oven to 350° Fahrenheit. Grease the pie plate with butter and set to the side for now.
3. Combine the filling ingredients and set aside.

4. Combine .25 cup of the sweetener, coconut flour, walnuts, flaxseed meal, and sea salt in a mixing dish.
5. Add the butter and mix until it's crumbly. Set about .5 of a cup aside and add another teaspoon of sweetener.
6. Add the crumbled mixture to the pie plate and spread it out until flattened.
7. Pour in the fruit mixture over the crust. Sprinkle with the rest of the crust fixings.
8. Bake for 20 minutes with a layer of foil. Remove and cook the last 10 to 20 minutes until browned.
9. When done, place in the fridge to set.
10. Slice and enjoy when it's firm.

Sugar-Free Slow-Cooked Fudge

Servings: 30
Total Prep & Cook Time: 3 hours (+) chill time
Total Macro Nutrients per Serving:
- 2 g Net Carbs
- 5 g Total Fats
- 1 g Total Protein
- 65 Calories

Fixings Needed:

- Sugar-free chocolate chips (2.5 cups)
- Vanilla liquid stevia – optional (2 tsp.)
- Coconut milk (.33 cup)
- Salt (1 pinch)
- Pure vanilla extract (1 tsp.)
- Recommended: 3-4-quart-size & 1-quart baking dish

Preparation Method:

1. Mix all of the fixings in the cooker. Close the lid and cook for two hours on the low setting.
2. Take the lid off and unplug the unit. *Don't stir* for 30 minutes to one hour.
3. Lastly, mix for five minutes until creamy smooth.
4. Line the baking dish with parchment paper. Spread the fudge into the plate, and chill until firm.

White Chocolate Bark

Servings: 12
Total Prep & Cook Time: 15-20 minutes
Total Macro Nutrients per Serving:
- -0- g Net Carbs
- 2.0 g Total Fats
- -0- g Total Protein
- 40 Calories

Fixings Needed:

- Cocoa butter (.25 cup)
- Low-carb sweetener (.33 cup)
- Vanilla powder (1 tsp.)
- Hemp seed powder (.5 tsp.)
- Toasted pumpkin seeds (1 tsp.)
- Salt (as desired)
- Coconut oil - for the bowl

Preparation Method:

1. Chop the cocoa butter into fine bits. Add water to a double boiler and add the pieces to melt using the medium heat setting. Stir in the rest of the fixings.
2. Lightly grease a bowl using a spritz of oil and add the mixture.
3. Let it cool and break into 12 portions.

CHAPTER 7

TIPS TO REMAIN IN KETOSIS

Keeping your diet in line takes a little effort. You now have tons of new snack recipes to help you along the right path. These are a few of the tips you can use daily to help keep your ketosis in line:

Make Healthier Choices On-The-Go:

When you have a busy lifestyle, it isn't always convenient to prepare your ketogenic snacks from scratch. Be a label checker and choose some of these options:

- Cacao Nibs: If you love chocolate chips; you will love the tasty nutrient-dense flavor of this low-carb treat. Just remember to count the carbs since they're so delicious - you may lose track of them.

- String Cheese: Select options without additional fillers.

- Full-Fat Laughing Cow Cheese Wheels: Enjoy *real* cheese when possible.

- Sardines: This zero-carb snack provides a healthy dose of fat and various other nutrients.

KETO SNACKS

- Beef Jerky: Choose ones with only a few additional ingredients. Be on the lookout for the added sugars.

- Pork Rinds: Use these to replace chips and crackers.

- Pickles: If you're craving something sour; grab a sugar-free pickle to consume some of the minerals your body is craving.

- Seaweed Snacks: Search the labels to make sure they do not contain significant amounts of oil.

Make Wise Drink Decisions:

The best choice is water, tea, coffee or sparkling water. Decaf coffee or herbal tea is another great option. If alcohol is your craving, choose dry wine, champagne, or light beer. Also, consider drinking the 'spirits' straight or with a bit of club soda.

Eliminate the Starches:

- Substitute with extra veggies or a salad to replace the starch.
- For a burger or sandwich – choose a lettuce wrap instead of a bun.

Add Healthy Fats:

- Add extra butter to the meat or veggies
- Use vinegar dressing or olive oil to drizzle over the meat and a salad.

You can always bring your own bottle of tasty oil with you, so you are sure to have the right mixture.

Dining Out Strategies:

When you make a choice to dine out; be smart and do some online research before you leave the house. Many of the restaurants have an online presence to make dieting a less daunting adventure. As you continue with your planning, it will become easier, and you can branch out to other locations with the knowledge gained. These are a few recommendations that might help:

- *A Healthy Breakfast:* Sometimes, there is nothing better than eggs if you want to play it safe. You may be off on some of the counts but after you have used some of the recipes in this book; you will know how to gauge your eating habits for the most important meal of the day.

- *A Delicious Lunch:* Fish and chicken are usually good choices. Try something like chicken salad or a regular salad. You need to beware of the dressing used. Try some vinaigrette or plain vinegar.

- *A Special Dinner:* Always choose a fresh green veggie with a lean cut of meat as your main course. Try something in the line of a hamburger minus the bun, or a tempting entrée of broccoli and steak.

Consider These Choices:

Panera Bread

Don't worry about the name of the shop; there are plenty of keto options. For example: Look at these options for a nice breakfast:

KETO SNACKS

- Power Breakfast Egg Bowl with Steak (3 grams)
- Power Breakfast Egg White Bowl with Roasted Turkey (4 grams)

Try lunch or dinner menus:

- Power Steak Lettuce Wraps (6 grams)
- Power Mediterranean Roasted Turkey Bowl (7 grams)
- Power Mediterranean Chicken (7 grams)

Denny's/Waffle House/IHOP

Dining out at a restaurant such as the above mentioned where breakfast is served all day, you may want to build your own. For example, Denny's offers a 'Build Your Own Grand Slam' where you can enjoy bacon and eggs on a budget. Choose some of these ingredients to create your own keto meal:

- Eggs
- Bacon
- Sausage
- Bacon
- Avocado
- Broccoli
- Spinach
- Cheese

Market Time: When you go to the supermarket, take your new skills, a grocery list, and read each of the labels.

Check Your Medications:

It's important to inform your doctor about your weight loss program. However, that doesn't mean you will need to eliminate the snacks. He/she may have prescribed some medicines that make you gain weight. These are a few to question:

- Insulin Injections: If taken in high doses, your insulin can impede weight loss. By consuming fewer carbs, you are substantially reducing the requirement of insulin. Again, ask your healthcare professional before you make any changes.

- Oral contraceptives
- Antidepressants
- Epilepsy drugs
- Blood pressure medications
- Allergy medicines
- Antibiotics

You need to remain diligent while on the kept-adapted diet plan since it can take several days to reach the keto state. One day of cheating can take your body a week to get back to ketosis. You may also gain water weight during the 'cheating' time.

If you are on the scales weekly and cheat, it is possible to see a four to six-pound weight gain even if you cheated five or six days ago. It will also take several more days for the weight loss to begin again.

Consistency begins with tracking the daily macros. The lists provide an additional layer of strictness to your diet. It makes you much more aware of the foods you consume in one day.

CONCLUSION

I hope you enjoyed each of the recipes provided in the *Keto Snacks: Sweet and Delicious Ketogenic & Low-Carb Diet – A Simple Keto Diet Cookbook for Beginners*. I also hope it was informative and provided you with all of the tools you need to achieve your goals whatever they may be.

The next step is to prepare your shopping list for your delicious snacks. Before you begin, you should consult your physician to ensure your body is ready for changes that will be included in the ketogenic plan. You may not like all of the foods on the plan, so you should be prepared to supplement your vitamins and minerals occasionally. These are some of the medications to consider:

- Greens/Veggie Supplements - The best way to get the greens in your keto diet is through meals such as spinach in your eggs or a low-carb veggie juice with a cheese snack. Have a salad with dinner. However, if you don't like greens; you can purchase a greens supplement. You can also add a measured scoop to a protein shake.

- Probiotics - You can eat Greek yogurt, kefir, kimchee, or similar fermented foods. You can also take a supplement.

- Electrolytes - You may experience some headaches, fatigue, or nausea which is sometimes called 'induction flu.' As you remove the carbs, your potassium and sodium (key electrolytes) are also removed. Taking a supplement will help with these issues.

- Sodium - You should receive at least one to two grams of extra sodium daily. Some of the pros accomplish this with bouillon cubes. Sea salt is a great option used in your diet plan.

KETO SNACKS

- Potassium - It is recommended to take supplements because potassium also leaves your body with salt. You can take 3 to 5 of the 99 mg tablets over-the-counter supplements.

- Vanadium and Chromium - These are both trace minerals which are essential to the production of insulin which will stabilize your body's blood sugar level.

- Malate or Magnesium Citrate - Help your diet plan along with regularity (constipation) while activating over 76% of the enzymatic processes in your body. You can take between 400 to 600 mg each day.

There are many more ways to supplement your diet while enjoying your snacks. If you're a beginner, you'll better understand how to make healthier choices as time passes.

www.ingramcontent.com/pod-product-compliance
Lightning Source LLC
Chambersburg PA
CBHW052054110526
44591CB00013B/2212